Contemporary Topics

ADVANCED

LISTENING

COMPREHENSION

David Beglar
Neil Murray

Series Editor
Michael Rost

Longman

Contemporary Topics: Advanced Listening Comprehension

Longman, 10 Bank Street, White Plains, N.Y. 10606

Associated companies:
Longman Group Ltd., London
Longman Cheshire Pty., Melbourne
Longman Paul Pty., Auckland
Copp Clark Pitman, Toronto

Photo Credits: Page 33, Giani L. Bellini/Leo de Wys, Inc.;
Page 41, Chester Higgins Jr./Photo Researchers, Inc.;
Page 49, Jerome Wexler/Photo Researchers, Inc.

Distributed in the United Kingdom by Longman Group
Ltd., Longman House, Burnt Mill, Harlow, Essex CM20
2JE, England and by associated companies, branches,
and representatives throughout the world.

Acquisitions director: Joanne Dresner
Development editor: Louisa Hellegers
Production editor: Lisa Hutchins
Text design: The Mazer Corporation
Cover design: Joseph DePinho
Text art: Woodshed Productions
Photo research: Woodshed Productions
Production supervisor: Anne Armeny

Library of Congress Cataloging-in-Publication Data

Beglar, David.
     Contemporary topics : advanced listening comprehension / David
Beglar, Neil Murray.
        p.   cm.— (Longman listening series)
     ISBN 0-8013-0928-X
     1. English language—Textbooks for foreign speakers.
2. Listening.   I. Murray, Neil (Neil L.)   II. Title. III. Series.
PE1128.B4189   1993
428.3'4 — dc20   92-39791
                                                         CIP

1 2 3 4 5 6 7 8 9 10-AL-96959493

CONTENTS

INTRODUCTION

This textbook was developed because of a number of problems we encountered in our own listening classes when instructing students in how to listen to lectures.

Our initial concern was to find a way to make lectures interesting, lively, and sometimes humorous—and appropriate for students at an advanced level. We were unable to find published materials that were both authentic and accessible to our students. Along with many of our colleagues, we knew that if we could not capture and hold the students' attention, we would never be able to help them maximize their learning. Our search led us to select from a wide range of academic topics that sparked our students' interest and curiosity.

In developing classroom activities to accompany the lectures, we rediscovered many of the fundamental principles of successful learning. Students need to be involved actively in each stage of the lesson; students need to develop an underlying *knowledge* of words and concepts that will help them comprehend new ideas and make inferences; students need opportunities to revise their study skills as they go through each lesson; and students need the expectation of a clear outcome in order to focus their efforts in each class.

What we eventually produced is the result of our efforts to find the right stuff—the right content and the right type of learning activities—to engage our students in the classroom and to prepare them for ever more challenging learning experiences in an English-speaking environment.

Our final concern in preparing this book was to make the learning stages in each unit as transparent as possible—both for you, the teacher, and for the student. As such, each section is prominently labeled and activities are clearly ordered. Although we encourage all instructors to remain flexible in planning how to use each unit in this textbook, we hope instructors and students alike will find the defined stages of each unit helpful.

In order to help instructors maximize the use of the textbook, we present the following brief explanation of some of our thinking regarding its various sections.

UNIT TITLE AND THEME PICTURE

Each unit opens with a title and photo or drawing that identifies the content area into which the unit fits. Even though the students will naturally look at this opening and draw some inferences about the content of the upcoming unit, it may be useful for you to take some class time to focus explicitly on the unit title and theme photo and have the students guess what kind of information may be covered in the lecture. Essentially, you can begin to draw on the knowledge the students already have about the topic at this time.

SECTION 1: TOPIC PREVIEW

The **Topic Preview** has two parts: a short reading and a number of questions (Warm-Up Discussion). Both parts serve the same purpose—to further draw the students into the topic and to predict the specific lecture content. The **Warm-Up Discussion** consists of some general questions and some very specific ones. The specific questions are directly covered in the lecture. Therefore, answering these questions will help students in their subsequent listening.

The questions may be answered in pairs or small groups of three to four students, or as a whole-class discussion activity. This section can be covered in roughly fifteen minutes, particularly if students have been instructed to look at the questions before class.

SECTION 2: VOCABULARY PREVIEW

Vocabulary learning has an important role in extended listening, and, as a result, it is dealt with in exercises both before and after the lecture. In the **Vocabulary Preview** section, twelve key vocabulary items are presented in a context similar to that in which they are found in the lecture. In this section, students first read the contextualized words and then check their comprehension in a simple test. This exercise normally requires about ten minutes of classroom time, but can be assigned as homework prior to the class meeting.

In addition, we have included a subsection titled **Word Networks** that includes other vocabulary items and also proper nouns that may be unfamiliar to the students. By offering an introductory presentation of new words in related groups, Word Networks is especially useful in preparing students for whom the material is very challenging. Word Networks is not presented as an explicit exercise or test, but rather as a reference for students before and after they listen to the lecture. You should allow five to ten minutes for this section; the students should read the words and ask you, or their classmates, about the expressions with which they are unfamiliar.

We recommend that you spend fifteen to thirty minutes of class time doing this vocabulary section, as time spent here provides important information regarding both the content and the organization of the lecture.

SECTION 3: LISTENING TO THE LECTURE

Because comprehending and remembering the details of a lecture in one listening is difficult to do, even for native speakers, students are asked to do multiple listenings of each lecture. However, the tasks vary with each listening.

In the beginning of Section 3 (**Before You Listen**), students are asked to predict some of the topics the speaker will deal with in the lecture. It is useful to elicit students' ideas and write them quickly on the chalkboard before the class listens to the lecture.

Lectures vary in length from nine to twelve minutes. Each lecture is divided into three or four sections; the sections average three minutes in length. The first recording of each lecture includes a **narrator** who introduces the lecture initially and then each section individually. The second recording has no narrator. The narrator assists the students, particularly during their first listening, by giving them a brief preview of the content in the upcoming section along with some clues regarding organization.

The **First Listening** section asks the students to listen to each part of the lecture and focus on main ideas. The students should read the question or questions provided before listening in order to help focus their attention as they listen. At the end of each section, you should stop the tape for about one minute to allow the students to answer the questions given.

The **Second Listening** section asks the students to listen again to each part of the lecture and to focus on facts and details that support the main idea. Again, the students should read the questions provided before listening in order to help focus their attention as they listen. For this listening, you may rewind the tape, or continue with the **second recording of the lecture**, which has no narrator.

The questions following the second listening are not intended to "test" the students on the lecture content, but rather to focus their listening on important points in the lecture that they may not have heard the first time.

When the questions have been answered, you may wish to have students first compare answers with their classmates in pairs or small groups. Then you can elicit the answers from the class as a whole. The answers are provided in **Appendix B**.

Section 3 is the central section of each unit and, since subsequent sections depend on an adequate comprehension of the lecture, it is important to spend ample class time with this section. The two listenings, with subsequent checking of the comprehension questions, will require about thirty minutes of class time.

SECTION 4: TAKING NOTES

Section 4 of the textbook helps the students improve their thinking skills, which in turn helps them in taking notes and retaining the lecture material.

The first part of Section 4 presents strategies and hints for note taking that can be used with lectures of the type presented in the unit. The second part of this section asks the students to listen again (preferably to the second recording of the lecture) and to take notes, attempting to use the hints and strategies given.

SECTION 5: REVIEWING THE CONTENT

In this section, students are asked to review their notes and prepare for the upcoming Review Test, much as they would have to do in an actual content class. They prepare, either individually or in small groups, by reviewing a short vocabulary list and answering several questions about main points in the lecture. This preparation may be done in class, but it may also be assigned as a homework activity.

The test itself should be taken in the class meeting *following* the review sessions in order to allow the students ample time to think about the material and to incorporate it into their long-term memory.

Review Tests are provided in **Appendix A**. Test formats vary, but usually involve a combination of factual questions, inference questions, and opinion questions. Most tests require no more than fifteen minutes of class time. Answers to the Review Tests are provided in **Appendix B**.

SECTION 6: PROJECTS

This is an application section. The projects that are suggested give the students an opportunity to use their knowledge of the topic in an active way. Using projects helps consolidate content learning and can provide expressive opportunities for all of the students in the class.

Two or three project options are given. The time required for each project will vary, so you or the students should choose projects that can realistically be done within the class meeting schedule.

THE LECTURES

The lectures are recorded in a "semi-authentic style." This means that they are based on unscripted lectures, but are edited to balance listening time with student activity time and rerecorded to improve sound quality.

However, the repairs and hesitations, as well as the tangential remarks and backtracking that are part of the style of natural discourse are preserved in the lectures.

The lectures average about ten minutes in length. Although this may seem long even to advanced-level students, students should not be made to feel a need to comprehend everything. Indeed, they should be encouraged to focus on learning to sift information, selecting key points, and dealing with gaps in received information.

The lectures are recorded twice. The first version is broken into parts corresponding to the ideas covered in the lecture. In this first version, a narrator gives a brief introduction to the upcoming section. This is done in order to help the students organize the information in the lecture. The second version of the lecture has no such breaks, and is, therefore, more difficult. Generally, the students will need to use the first version as a first listening, in conjunction with the questions in Section 3, but will use the second version during subsequent review listenings.

THE LECTURE SCRIPTS

The transcript for each lecture appears in the back of the textbook in **Appendix C**. This transcript is to be used by you, as needed to prepare for teaching each unit. It can also be used by the class, following the Review Test, for verification of lecture information and for further study of vocabulary and rhetorical patterns.

Obviously, the transcript should not be used by the students as they do the exercises in the unit or prepare for the Review Test as this undermines the development of listening and study skills. If student use of the transcripts becomes a problem, it may be best for you to remove the transcript pages from the students' books.

THE FINAL FACTOR: USE OF TEACHER INTUITION

While trying to give meaningful guidance to you, the teacher, in this introduction, we have avoided dense explanations in order to leave room for your own intuition, flexibility, and creativity in teaching. Although we hope the suggestions here have helped you prepare for teaching this course, we also hope that you will find your own

teaching strategies and use your own insights into your students' learning in order to maximize the effectiveness of this material.

TO THE STUDENT

When you begin studying in an English-speaking environment, you will find yourself in many "lecture situations." You will have to pay attention and listen for long periods of time. At first, you may feel overwhelmed by the speed and content level of the lectures you have to listen to. This is a very natural reaction!

Many students receive little or no practice dealing with this kind of lecture situation. They have to learn by the sink-or-swim approach. (If you don't sink, you will somehow learn to swim.) This textbook was designed to give you another approach, so that you don't have to risk sinking! There is no mystery in learning to listen to lectures—but there is a lot of preparation you have to do and some strategies (or ways of thinking) that you will have to learn. Of course, this is hard work, but it can be enjoyable at the same time.

This textbook presents twelve lectures that are similar to the kind of introductory lectures you will find in content classes. They are natural in their language style, speed of delivery, and depth of subject matter.

Each lecture is surrounded by different kinds of exercises to help you learn to listen. Because listening is basically an active thinking skill, you will be very active when you use this textbook.

Here are some of the activities:
- Discussing and sharing ideas
- Working with vocabulary
- Predicting main ideas
- Listening and taking notes
- Analyzing your notes
- Thinking about and discussing the ideas in the lecture
- Preparing for tests and taking tests
- Applying what you learn in project work

You will be doing some of these activities individually (on your own), some in small groups, and some as a whole class. All of these exercises require your active participation and your belief in your own ability to learn.

We wish you luck and we hope you enjoy this course.

THE WORLD OF COMICS

THE FAR SIDE

"Mr. Osborne, may I be excused? My brain is full."

1 TOPIC PREVIEW

What do you think is the most popular part of an American newspaper? The front page?
The editorial section? The sports section? The comics? If your answer was "comics," you
are correct. More people read the comics section than any other part of the paper. Everyone can enjoy comics because they can make us smile, involve us in the drama of an
unfolding story, and occasionally even give us quick insight into current social and political issues.

WARM-UP DISCUSSION

In groups, discuss these topics with your classmates.

1. How often do you read the newspaper? What sections of the newspaper do you
   usually read?
2. Do you read the comics sometimes? If so, which ones do you like?
3. What are the names of two popular comic strips in your country?
4. Can you name some common types of comics?

2 VOCABULARY PREVIEW

Read the following sentences. Circle the letter of the word or phrase that is closest in meaning to the *italicized* expression.

1. Many people read the comics section for *entertainment* and not for any serious reason.
   a. education
   b. information
   c. enjoyment
   d. practice

2. Many characters in the comics are *funny-looking*. We smile when we see them.
   a. serious
   b. humorous
   c. interesting
   d. political

3. Some comics look very *realistic*. They are drawn in a lifelike manner.
   a. have accurate details
   b. are very poorly drawn
   c. are very entertaining
   d. make people laugh

4. Some comics resemble *soap operas* on afternoon television. They deal with the good and bad things people do.
   a. musical plays
   b. political documentaries
   c. dramas about people's lives
   d. "clean" programs for children

5. John draws *satirical comics* for the school newspaper that attack the government's decisions rather humorously.
   a. comics that are detailed
   b. comics that make you laugh
   c. comics that are exciting
   d. comics that use humor to criticize

6. Since the topic of this comic strip is *politics*, its drawings often include presidents and other world leaders.
   a. government
   b. world society
   c. important people
   d. rich people

7. *Current trends* are often reflected in comic strips. These topics are both timely and discussed by many people.
   a. new products
   b. serious problems
   c. up-to-date ideas
   d. topics more than ten years old

8. The *plots* of some comic strips are hard to follow. You have to read these comics every day in order to know what has been happening.
   a. character development
   b. origins
   c. fictions
   d. story lines

9. Some comic strips have a very large *audience*. Many people like to read them.
   a. number of editors
   b. number of characters
   c. number of readers
   d. number of writers

10. The *primary* purpose of many comics is to make people laugh. Many people read the comics only for enjoyment.
   a. most interesting
   b. imaginary
   c. main
   d. least important

11. Some comics use *sarcasm* in order to criticize famous people. These comics appear to be funny, but are actually critical.
   a. bitter, mocking language
   b. simple, humorous language
   c. joyful, positive language
   d. angry, confused language

12. Some comics contain *violence*. There is always a lot of fighting and threatening others with the use of guns.
   a. the use of humor to entertain someone
   b. the use of money to influence someone
   c. the use of force to injure someone
   d. the use of words to confuse someone

W O R D   N E T W O R K S

These are some words and phrases you will hear in the lecture. Read the list. Ask about and discuss the words or phrases you do not know.

Major newspapers
New York Times
Wall Street Journal

Names of comics
Hogan's Alley
Peanuts
Little Orphan Annie
Doonesbury
Bloom County
Dick Tracy
Mary Worth

Characters in comic strips
Snoopy
Charlie Brown

Types of comics
humorous comics
satirical comics
adventure comics
dramatic comics

Some terms to talk about comics
characters
backgrounds
everyday things
unexpected things
identify with
topics
humorous comments
political views
political injustice
romance
human relationships

3 LISTENING TO THE LECTURE

BEFORE YOU LISTEN

You are going to listen to a lecture about comics. Think about some of the topics that might be mentioned. Write down two topics that the speaker might cover.

1._____

2._____

FIRST LISTENING: MAIN IDEAS

Listen to each part of the lecture to find out the main ideas. Circle a, b, or c.

PART 1

PEANUTS reprinted by permission of UFS, Inc.

1. A good title for Part 1 might be:
   a. How Comics Are Named
   b. The Early History of Comics
   c. The Most Popular Comics

PART 2

DOONESBURY copyright 1974 G. B. Trudeau. Reprinted with permission of UNIVERSAL PRESS SYNDICATE. All rights reserved.

1. What types of comics are described in this section?
   a. satirical and action comics
   b. satirical and adventure comics
   c. satirical and violent comics

PART 3

Reprinted with special permission of North American Syndicate, Inc.

1. What are the main themes of dramatic comics?
   a. romance and human relationships
   b. murder and suspense
   c. war and business

SECOND LISTENING: FACTS AND DETAILS

Listen to each part of the lecture again. This time listen to learn more facts and details. Answer the questions below. Write T (true) or F (false) in front of each sentence.

PART 1

1. _____ Every newspaper in the United States has comics.

2. _____ The first popular comic strip in the United States was *Peanuts*.

3. _____ Humorous comics usually have simple backgrounds.

PART 2

1. _____ Satirical comics mix humor and serious topics.

2. _____ Characters in satirical comics are usually simply drawn.

3. _____ *Dick Tracy* is a good example of a satirical comic.

PART 3

1. _____ Dramatic comics are very different from TV soap operas.

2. _____ *Mary Worth* is a well-known adventure comic.

3. _____ Comics will probably disappear from newspapers soon.

4 TAKING NOTES

MAIN IDEAS AND SUPPORTING FACTS

Read the information below and discuss it with your classmates.

There are two main purposes for taking lecture notes:

1. Taking notes can help us *concentrate*.
2. Taking notes gives us information that we can *review* later.

Especially for the purpose of review, taking *organized notes* is very important.

Well-organized notes should be arranged in the kind of format that we use for *making an outline*. This means that the *main topics* and the *main ideas* should be on the left-hand side of the page; the *supporting facts, examples,* and *details* should be moved slightly to the right.

This is illustrated with sample notes below.

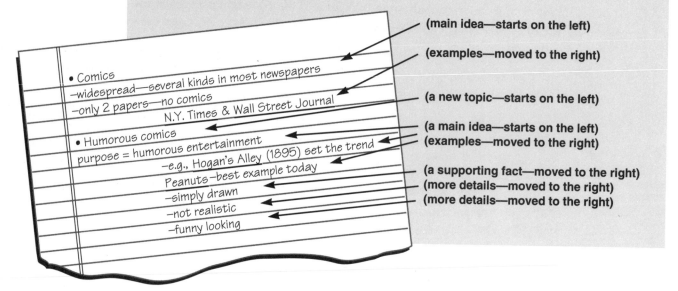

- Comics
  —widespread—several kinds in most newspapers
  —only 2 papers—no comics
            N.Y. Times & Wall Street Journal
- Humorous comics
  purpose = humorous entertainment
            —e.g., Hogan's Alley (1895) set the trend
          Peanuts—best example today
            —simply drawn
            —not realistic
            —funny looking

(main idea—starts on the left)

(examples—moved to the right)

(a new topic—starts on the left)

(a main idea—starts on the left)
(examples—moved to the right)

(a supporting fact—moved to the right)
(more details—moved to the right)
(more details—moved to the right)

ORGANIZING YOUR NOTES

Now listen to the lecture again and take notes. Try to organize your notes as you write. Write the main ideas *on the left* and the supporting facts, examples, and details *to the right*.

REVIEWING THE CONTENT

DESCRIPTION

This lecture gives you a lot of information about comics — the styles and themes in different types of comics. This kind of information is called *description* because it describes the features or characteristics of a topic. In a lecture that gives you a lot of description, it is important to note the main *descriptive words* and *phrases*.

USING YOUR NOTES

Look at the lecture notes you have just written. Describe the following types of comics to a classmate. Use your own words. You may *use* your notes, but *don't read* from them.

1. Humorous comics
2. Satirical comics
3. Adventure comics
4. Dramatic comics

PREPARING FOR THE TEST

In your next class, you will take a short test on the lecture. Before taking the test, be sure to review the following questions. Use your notes as you review. You will not be able to use your notes during the test.

1. Do you know the words in *italics?* Write a similar word or a brief definition.
   a. People read comics for *entertainment.*
   b. Some types of comics look very *realistic.*
   c. *Satirical comics* often deal with political issues.
   d. *Humorous comics* are quite common.
   e. Dramatic comics resemble *soap operas.*
   f. *Politics* are a common topic of some comics.

2. How did comics become popular in the United States?
3. What types of comics are mentioned in the lecture?
4. Give examples of each type of comics.

REVIEW: FINAL LISTENING

Now listen one last time to the lecture. Follow your notes as you listen. Think about the descriptions that are given by the lecturer. If you still have any questions about the lecture, ask your teacher.

TAKING THE TEST

If you have reviewed the material, you should be ready to take the Review Test. Turn to page 97 and answer the questions. Do *not* use your notes.

PROJECTS

Try these projects after you have finished the Review Test.

1. Bring the comics section of a local newspaper to class. Then get together in groups and label the comics according to type. Try to find examples of each of the following types of comics: humorous, satirical, adventure, and dramatic. When you have finished, show them to another group and explain the reasons for your choices.

2. Choose two of the four types of comic strips mentioned in question 1 and write a short, original comic strip of your own. Make copies and share them with the other students in your class.

3. In the lecture on comics, one type of comic was not spoken about — that is, political cartoons — cartoons that use current situations in society and government. Try to find some examples of political cartoons. Bring them to class. What do you think is the purpose of a political cartoon?

THE KEYS TO ADVERTISING

1 TOPIC PREVIEW

Most of us see dozens of advertisements every single day. They are found in the newspapers and magazines that we read, the radio programs we listen to, and the television programs we watch. Advertisers, and the companies that create the advertising, are constantly looking for new ways to catch the public's attention. One type of advertisement that has been particularly successful in attracting customers uses famous rock stars to promote products.

WARM-UP DISCUSSION

In groups, discuss these topics with your classmates.

1. Describe an advertisement that you remember very well. Why did the ad make such a strong impression on you?
2. Why do companies advertise?
3. How do advertisers try to make products attractive to people?
4. Have you seen any advertisements today? Where did you see them?
5. Have you ever seen an advertisement with a famous person in it? Was it effective? Why or why not?

9

2 VOCABULARY PREVIEW

Read the following sentences and try to guess the meaning of the words in *italics*.

1. The best way to *promote* a product is through frequent advertising. This pushes the idea into people's minds.
2. Repeating the same ad frequently is a good *technique* for increasing sales.
3. Interesting, exciting, or persuasive ads can be very *convincing*. People begin to believe the ad is true.
4. We see advertising every day in many places. It's *pervasive* in the United States.
5. Companies *focus on* selling to young people by using rock stars in their ads. The rock stars help the companies make their products appeal to young people.
6. Companies concerned with *prestige* generally sell very expensive, fancy products.
7. Often we *are influenced by* people we like or respect very much. We try to do things that they do.
8. Some companies *target* specific ethnic groups with their advertising. They try to interest particular groups with their ads.
9. Since music tours are so expensive, it's helpful for groups to have *sponsors*. A sponsor helps to pay for the costs.
10. A *major distinction* must be made between effective and ineffective advertising.
11. If a product is becoming less popular, advertising can help to *reinforce* sales.
12. *Consumers* are attracted by interesting, creative ads. They will spend their money more easily if they are interested in the ad.

Now fill in the blanks in the sentences below. Use the correct form of the words from above.

1. Advertising is _____pervasive_____ in American society. It's on TV and radio, in newspapers and magazines, and on billboards.

2. _____ are often big companies who want to get publicity.

3. Rolls Royce advertisements try to _____ only wealthy people.

4. Many advertisements _____ the ideas of activeness, attraction, and youth.

5. Jewelry and designer clothing ads are often concerned with the idea of

_____ .

6. Often, people's ideas about products _____ the ads they see. Although they may not always realize it, ads can change their thinking.

7. Companies use special _____ to make their advertisements exciting, interesting, and persuasive.

8. Ads can _____ ideas as well as products.

9. Making _____ advertisements is quite difficult. Changing people's opinions or favorite products is not easy.

10. Companies advertise because they want _____ to buy their products.

11. If a product is becoming less popular, effective and heavy advertising can help

    _____ its sales.

12. There is a _____ between advertising on national television and advertising in a small newspaper. There are many differences between the two.

W O R D   N E T W O R K S

These are some words and phrases you will hear in the lecture. Read the list.
Ask about and discuss any words or phrases you do not know.

Ideas related to advertising
message transmission
media
printed
audio
audiovisual
personal satisfaction
socially acceptable
personally attractive
incredible effect

Advertising terms
appeals
attracts the customer's attention
main selling point
factual appeal
emotional appeal
slogans
"Reeboks let U.B.U." (a slogan)
testimonials
repetition
promotional idea

Names
Michael Jackson
Reebok
Amnesty International
Bruce Springsteen
Tracy Chapman
Sting
Pepsi
"Billy Jean"
Hispanics
Gloria Estefan and Miami Sound
  Machine
Whitney Houston
Diet Coke

3 LISTENING TO THE LECTURE

BEFORE YOU LISTEN

You are going to listen to a lecture about advertising techniques. Can you predict two of the topics that you think will be discussed in this lecture?

1._____

2._____

FIRST LISTENING: MAIN IDEAS

Listen to each part of the lecture to find out the main ideas. Circle a, b, or c.

PART 1

1. According to the lecture, what does advertising need to do in order to be successful?
   a. to affect society through the use of advertising techniques
   b. to attract people's attention and give them reasons to buy a product
   c. to promote the sales of products and increase company profits

PART 2

1. What are the two types of appeal in advertising?
   a. informational and personal
   b. common and prestige
   c. factual and emotional

2. What is a slogan?
   a. the name of the product being sold
   b. a short phrase used to promote a product
   c. a song used to advertise a product

PART 3

1. What is a testimonial?
   a. an ad in which a person says he or she likes a product
   b. an ad in which a famous song is used to sell a product
   c. an ad in which a specific group of people is targeted

2. What is repetition?
   a. using the same person in several different commercials
   b. playing the same advertisement many times
   c. advertising different products using a variety of media

SECOND LISTENING: FACTS AND DETAILS

Listen to each part of the lecture again. This time listen to learn more facts and details. Answer the questions below. Write T (true) or F (false) in front of each sentence.

PART 1

1. _____ Advertising is used only to promote products.

2. _____ Advertising is a $19 billion a year industry.

3. _____ Advertising is done mainly in newspapers and magazines.

PART 2

1. _____ A factual appeal presents information about a product.

2. _____ Ads with rock stars generally use factual appeals.

3. _____ A good slogan should be basically simple.

PART 3

1. _____ Testimonials are a way of showing support for a product.

2. _____ Pepsi has used rock stars to target ethnic groups.

3. _____ Advertisers believe that the more often we see or hear an ad, the more we'll want their product.

4 TAKING NOTES

INTRODUCTION TO ABBREVIATIONS AND SYMBOLS

Read the information below and discuss it with your classmates.

When we take notes, it is important to write quickly and efficiently. One way to increase our note-taking speed is to use *abbreviations* and *symbols*. There are many standard abbreviations (for example, hour = hr.), but we are free to use our own abbreviations. We may also cut out some words altogether, especially function words (for example, *to, of, for,* etc.).

Look at the sample notes below. You will find unabbreviated notes on the left side, and notes with abbreviations and symbols on the right. Compare the two. What is different about them?

Advertising is a message designed to promote a product, service, or idea.	Advertising—message designed to promote a prod. , serv. , idea
* ninety billion dollar industry in the United States	* $90 bil. industry in U.S.
* big effect on society	* big effect on soc.
* found in newspapers, magazines, TV, radio	* found in news., mags, TV, radio
* successful advertising does two things:	* successful adver. –> 2 things:
• First—attracts attention; is interesting	• 1—attracts attn. – is interesting
• Second—gives reasons for buying	• 2—gives reasons for buying
* Testimonials—advertisements that have people tell they use and like certain products	* testimonials—ads.—people use & like prods.
• rock star testimonials— effective way to influence young people	•rock strs.—effective way to infl. yng. peo.
• can say this directly or imply by their actions	•can say or imply

USING THE OUTLINE FORMAT

Now listen to the lecture again and take notes. Use the outline format — main ideas on the left, minor ideas under them on the right. Also, use abbreviations and symbols when you can. When you finish taking notes, go back and circle any abbreviations you made.

5 REVIEWING THE CONTENT

DEFINITION

When giving lectures, teachers may use some difficult words and phrases. Sometimes the speaker will give a brief definition of words to help you understand new or difficult words, especially if the new words are *key terms* that you need to understand the lecture fully.

USING YOUR NOTES

Work with a classmate. Look at your notes and complete the following definitions.

1. *Advertising* is _____

2. The basis of all techniques is the *appeal,* which is _____

3. A *factual appeal* tells how _____

4. An *emotional appeal* focuses on how _____

5. A *slogan* is _____

6. *Testimonials* are _____

7. *Repetition* means _____

PREPARING FOR THE TEST

In your next class, you will take a short test on the lecture. Before taking the test, be sure to review the following questions. Use your notes as you review. You will not be able to use your notes during the test.

1. Can you use these words in sentences?
   - **a.** promote
   - **b.** factual appeal
   - **c.** emotional appeal
   - **d.** slogan
   - **e.** testimonials
   - **f.** sponsor
   - **g.** repetition
   - **h.** consumers

2. What is the main purpose of advertising?
3. What two things does advertising need to do in order to be successful?
4. Give two reasons why rock stars help make ads effective.

REVIEW: FINAL LISTENING

Now listen one last time to the lecture. Follow your notes as you listen.

TAKING THE TEST

Turn to page 98 and answer the questions. Do *not* use your notes.

PROJECTS

Try these projects after you have finished the Review Test.

1. Work in groups of four or five people. Discuss the pros and cons of rock musicians or other stars selling and advertising products. Is it "too commercial" or just a good business decision?

2. Find an ad in a newspaper or magazine or on video that features a music star. Is it an effective ad? Who would be most influenced by it? Present a summary to the class.

3. Role play: In pairs or small groups, write a script and then act out a commercial that uses a song to promote a product. Remember to have the song playing in the background during your commercial.

COMPUTER CRIME

1 TOPIC PREVIEW

Computer crime has become a problem of the 1990s that is likely to continue far into the future. Computer criminals are often quite different from other kinds of criminals. According to some experts, these criminals seem to lock themselves away from other people and live in their own fantasy "microworlds." They are also generally quite young. They break into others' computers in order to steal, add, or change information. For many of them, this is a kind of game, a part of their fantasy life. However, it is a dangerous "game," and, as a result, many individuals and corporations are very concerned about computer security.

WARM-UP DISCUSSION

In groups, discuss these topics with your classmates.

1. Do you use a computer regularly? If you do, could someone "steal" important information from your computer?

2. Do you ever use a "bank computer" — a cash card machine at a bank — to withdraw money? What would you do if you found someone stealing money from the machine by using a secret code?

3. Have you ever heard of a case of computer crime? What happened? Was the criminal caught?

VOCABULARY PREVIEW

Read the following sentences and try to guess the meaning of the words in *italics*.

1. Stealing money or secret information are examples of *crimes,* and people who do such things are punished if they are caught.
2. The bank manager tried to *cover up* the fact that he was stealing money.
3. By *gaining access to* the computer, he was able to change some data.
4. Companies concerned with *financial* business control large amounts of money daily and so rely heavily on computers to help them with their work.
5. His stealing the software was purely *malicious.* His only gain was a feeling of revenge; the software itself was useless to him.
6. After my computer was destroyed by the fire, I called my *insurance company.*
7. The company has *secret information* in its computer files. It doesn't want anyone to see this information.
8. Changing the data on your company's computer in order to get a higher pay check is an example of *fraud.*
9. People who break the law often have to go to *court,* where they are judged.
10. It was a terrible *tragedy* for him when all his expensive computer equipment was smashed during the earthquake.
11. If the computer *scrambles* the information, we won't be able to understand it unless we know the correct code.
12. Einstein was a scientific *genius.* His ideas were much more advanced than those of the other scientists of his time.

Now match each word with its correct definition.

1. ___i___ court
2. _____ crimes
3. _____ financial
4. _____ genius
5. _____ gaining access to
6. _____ insurance company
7. _____ secret information
8. _____ malicious
9. _____ scrambles
10. _____ tragedy
11. _____ cover up
12. _____ fraud

a. a dishonest activity done to get money
b. any acts that are against the law
c. a terrible or unhappy event
d. connected with money
e. hide
f. mixes up
g. entering
h. a company that has agreed to pay money in case of misfortune, such as illness, accident, or death
i. a place where legal cases are heard and judged
j. wishing to hurt other people
k. data concealed or hidden from others
l. a person with extraordinary intellectual power

W O R D   N E T W O R K S

These are some words and phrases you will hear in the lecture. Read the list.
Ask about and discuss any words or phrases you do not know.

Computer terms
computer networks
hackers
transfers
passwords
allow access
directory
scrambling devices
scrambling key
audit trail software
audit trails

Names
War Games (a movie)
Memorial Sloan-Kettering Cancer
   Center

Business
statistics
business organizations
inventory
sales figures
financially motivated

Crime and crime prevention
dangerous
opportunities for crime
computerized military defense system
military security
significant rewards
out for gain
hardest hit by
detected
financial disaster
theft
preventing

Medicine
medical equipment
patients' records
treatment

3 LISTENING TO THE LECTURE

BEFORE YOU LISTEN

You are now going to hear a lecture about computer crime. Think about what position the speaker might take — will the speaker think computer crime is a serious problem or not such a serious problem?

Your answer:

_____

FIRST LISTENING: MAIN IDEAS

Listen to each part of the lecture to find out the main ideas. Circle a, b, or c.

PART 1

1. Why are the police concerned about computer crime?
   a. Computer users are gaining access to police computers.
   b. Computer users are getting private or secret information.
   c. They don't have enough people to work on all the crimes.

PART 2

1. According to the lecture, most computer hacking is probably done
   a. for malicious reasons.
   b. for financial or material gain.
   c. for the fun or challenge of it.

2. According to the lecture
   a. certain kinds of companies suffer greatly from computer crime.
   b. all hacking is done to make money.
   c. officials do not believe hackers can cause a major financial disaster.

PART 3

1. What is being done in order to stop hacking?
   a. Courts are being tougher on computer hackers.
   b. Companies are investigating and selecting their employees more carefully.
   c. New types of computers are being manufactured.

SECOND LISTENING: FACTS AND DETAILS

Listen to each part of the lecture again. This time listen to learn more facts and details. Answer the questions below. Write T (true) or F (false) in front of each sentence.

PART 1

1. _____ The number of computer criminals has been increasing.

2. _____ Computer crime is the subject of a movie called *War Games.*

3. _____ Computer crime is tempting because it is challenging and because the criminal may gain significant rewards.

PART 2

1. _____ Insurance companies are seldom targets for hackers.

2. _____ More than $40 million are transferred over America's financial networks every day.

3. _____ In 1983, a hacker gained access to a hospital computer's memory and the incident ended in tragedy.

PART 3

1. _____ "Dial back" systems use passwords.

2. _____ Scrambling devices prevent hackers from gaining access to a computer.

3. _____ Only audit trail software is completely satisfactory as a computer security system.

4 TAKING NOTES

KEY WORDS AND PHRASES

Read the information below and discuss it with your classmates.

The *key words* from a lecture will help you remember the main themes and ideas. Therefore, it is important to include key words and phrases in your notes.

Below are a number of key words and phrases that have been taken from Part 1 of the lecture. Look at them for a moment and see if you can recall this section of the lecture.

computers becoming popular
opportunities for crime
access private, secret information
dangerous—movie War Games
significant rewards

CHECKING YOUR NOTES

Now listen to the lecture again and take notes. After you have taken notes on the entire lecture, circle the key words and phrases. Compare your key words and phrases with a classmate's.

REVIEWING THE CONTENT

CAUSE-AND-EFFECT

Cause-and-effect thinking is one of the most common forms of logic that we use in social sciences and natural sciences. In these sciences, we discuss the *reasons* for actions and the *results* of actions. These reasons and results are known as *causes* and *effects.*

When you listen, thinking about cause-and-effect patterns can help you understand possible reasons for events, attitudes, beliefs, and behaviors. Typical questions that are often answered by cause-and-effect arguments are:

1. What are the causes of X?
2. What are the consequences of X?
3. What would happen to X if . . . ?
4. What is the effect of X?

USING YOUR NOTES

Look at your notes. Complete these cause-and-effect relationships.

1. Computer crime is tempting *because*_____

2. Courts are being tougher on computer criminals *in an effort to*_____

3. The use of passwords *can prevent* computer crime *by* _____

4. Computer engineers are *developing* access control software *in order to*_____

5. *The effect* of these changes has been _____

PREPARING FOR THE TEST

In your next class you will take a short test on the ideas in the lecture. Before taking the test, use your notes and answer the following questions.

1. Do you understand the following words? Can you use them in sentences?
   a. gain access to
   b. malicious
   c. insurance companies
   d. fraud
   e. theft
   f. financially motivated
   g. tragedy
   h. scrambling devices

2. What are the different reasons that hackers break into computer networks?
3. What are some of the ways in which the police and businesses are trying to fight computer crime?

REVIEW: FINAL LISTENING

Now listen one last time to the lecture. Follow your notes as you listen.

TAKING THE TEST

Turn to page 99 and answer the questions. Do *not* use your notes.

PROJECTS

Try these projects after you have finished the Review Test.

1. Look up *hacking* in an encyclopedia, or bring in a newspaper or magazine article dealing with this topic. Note down any information the encyclopedia or article gives you that was not in the lecture you heard. Share this information with your class.

2. Consider some of the potential targets for hackers. Complete the table below.

TARGET	CAUSE	EFFECT
Bank	To get money	Damage to their business Loss of customer confidence
School or university		
Medical research company		
Police headquarters		
Stock company		

MEMORY: OUR KEY TO LEARNING

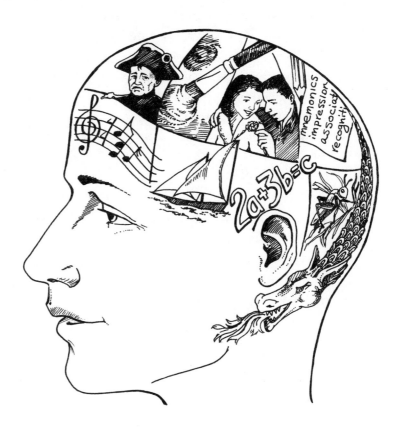

1 TOPIC PREVIEW

Most of us take our memory for granted. We almost never stop to think about how important memory is to our lives. But think about this: If you remembered nothing from the past, you would be unable to learn anything new. All of your experiences would be lost as soon as they ended, and every new situation would be completely unfamiliar.

Psychologists are learning more every day about what happens when we store new memories. They now know about some of the changes that take place in the brain's nerve cells when we try to store or retrieve "items" in or from our memory. Certainly, as psychologists and neurologists find out more about the workings of the brain, the secrets of memory will become clearer.

WARM-UP DISCUSSION

In groups, discuss these topics with your classmates.

1. Do you have a good memory? Why do you say "yes" or "no"?
2. Do you think we have different types of memory? If so, what are they?
3. How could you measure a person's memory? What kinds of tests would you give a person to measure his or her memory?
4. How do you remember things? Do you use any special techniques?

2 VOCABULARY PREVIEW

Read the following sentences. Circle the letter of the word or phrase that is closest in meaning to the *italicized* expression.

1. Dr. Sigmund Freud was one of the first doctors to study ***psychology.*** He wanted to explain how people thought and why they desired different things.
    a. the study of language
    b. the study of the mind
    c. the study of economics
    d. the study of the human body

2. The ***duration*** of a memory can vary. Some of us remember for only a short time and others for our whole lives.
    a. intensity
    b. length of time
    c. logic
    d. importance

3. When they wake up, many people cannot ***recall*** their dreams. Other people can ***recall*** them just long enough to write them down.
    a. understand
    b. remember
    c. talk about
    d. think about

4. The ***retina*** is necessary if we are to see. It receives images formed by the lens. The ***retina*** is also connected to the brain via the optic nerve.
    a. a part of the brain
    b. a part of the eye
    c. a part of the ear
    d. a part of the spine

5. Information can be ***stored*** in our brains for many years. It is waiting there to be used.
    a. kept; held
    b. lost; misplaced
    c. forgotten
    d. needed; wanted

6. The ***mnemonic HOMES*** helped the students remember the names of the Great Lakes in the United States: *H*uron, *O*ntario, *M*ichigan, *E*rie and *S*uperior.
    a. a memory aid that, for example, uses the first letter of a series of words
    b. a word spelled with all capital letters
    c. a method of testing memory used throughout the world
    d. a type of code used by many students

7. Psychologists can ***classify*** memory into several categories.
    a. separate
    b. define
    c. eliminate
    d. discuss

8. Students often try to ***memorize*** material just before a test. They study it until they know the words exactly.
    a. completely forget
    b. briefly look at
    c. talk about
    d. remember perfectly

9. Sometimes we need to *rearrange* a list of words in order to make it more organized. Putting similar words together is useful.
   a. write clearly
   b. discuss
   c. change the order of
   d. erase

10. The information in our brains is not *random.* It is well organized and interconnected.
   a. easy to remember
   b. complex
   c. without plan or pattern
   d. the same for all people

11. One *essential* feature of our memories is that they are organized. Without this feature, our brains could not function properly.
   a. unimportant
   b. interesting
   c. necessary
   d. surprising

12. Some memories are *temporary* because we don't consider them important, and we don't remember them very long.
   a. sad to think about
   b. extremely accurate
   c. difficult to understand
   d. lasting for a limited time

WORD NETWORKS

These are some words and phrases you will hear in the lecture. Read the list. Ask about and discuss any words or phrases you do not know.

Terms from psychology
sensory memory
short-term memory
long-term memory
impression
senses
sensation
fades
visual information
visual cortex
sensitive to light patterns
temporary storage
visualizing
limited
considerable lengths of time
preserve meaning
recognition
relearning
mnemonics
associate
recognize
personalizing
organization
logical

Terms from psychology experiments
lighted match
sparkler
word list
recognition test
geography
Great Lakes
Midwest
techniques
diameter
unrelated words

3 LISTENING TO THE LECTURE

BEFORE YOU LISTEN

You are going to listen to a lecture on memory. What do you think is the first topic the speaker will discuss?

_____

FIRST LISTENING: MAIN IDEAS

Listen to each part of the lecture to find out the main ideas. Circle a, b, or c.

PART 1

1. Memory is generally divided into how many types?
   a. It's not divided. There's basically only one type.
   b. three types
   c. more types than we can count

2. What does sensory memory do?
   a. It recalls what we see, hear, taste, touch, and smell.
   b. It holds information gained only from the sense of touch.
   c. It keeps memories we had as babies.

PART 2   44 + 8 + 10 + 18 = ??

You need to use your short-term memory to understand this sentence!

1. How long does short-term memory hold information?
   a. one to twenty seconds
   b. less than twenty minutes
   c. as long as you think about something

2. What is the primary focus of long-term memory?
   a. words people say
   b. things we sense
   c. meaning

PART 3   **Word List**

tuba	badminton	circle	orchid
drum	baseball	rectangle	iris
piano	tennis	square	rose
guitar	basketball	triangle	lily
flute	football	oval	daisy

1. Recall is
   a. remembering information.
   b. writing down information.
   c. learning information for the second time.

2. Recognition is
   a. remembering a person's exact words.
   b. remembering if you have seen something before.
   c. remembering something from a very long time ago.

PART 4   **12,754 kilometers**

1. Which of the following is not a way to improve your memory?
    a. organize ideas
    b. relate ideas to your life
    c. use songs and poems to remember things

2. Memory techniques are ways of
    a. associating information with something we know.
    b. using all of our memories.
    c. making all information seem very important.

bear — *kuma*	sun — *taiyo*
earth — *chikyu*	moon — *tsuki*
lily — *yuri*	tiger — *tora*
moon — *tsuki*	wolf — *okami*
wolf— *okami*	rose — *bara*
rose — *bara*	lily — *yuri*

SECOND LISTENING: FACTS AND DETAILS

Listen to each part of the lecture again. This time listen to learn more facts and details. Answer the questions below. Write T (true) or F (false) in front of each sentence.

PART 1

1. _____ Memory has been intensively researched.
2. _____ Memory can be classified by time or duration of use.
3. _____ Sensory memory lasts approximately five seconds.

PART 2

1. _____ Short-term memory is like a temporary storage place for information.
2. _____ Short-term memory is rarely necessary for reading.
3. _____ Information stored for longer than a minute is in long-term memory.

PART 3

1. _____ We use recall many times every day.
2. _____ Recognition is generally more difficult than recall.
3. _____ Seeing how quickly we can memorize something a second time is called retrieval.

PART 4

1. _____ There are many types of mnemonics.
2. _____ The lecturer used the technique of retrieval to remember the circumference of the Earth.
3. _____ Our minds store information in a basically random way.

4 TAKING NOTES

LISTING AND ENUMERATING

Read the information below and discuss it with your classmates.

When we take notes, we organize things into logical groups. We put information of the same kind, or talk about the same thing, together. We sometimes make lists of related information. *Listing* and *enumerating* help us to understand and remember information better. In the lecture on memory, the lecturer speaks about three things having to do with memory:

- 3 types of memory
- 3 ways of measuring memory
- 3 ways of improving memory

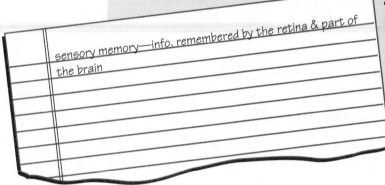

USING LISTS

Now listen to the lecture again and complete the list below (or use your notebook). The first one has been started for you. Remember to use abbreviations wherever possible.

3 types of memory:

a. sensory memory — info. remembered by the retina & part of the brain

b.

c.

3 ways of measuring memory:

a.

b.

c.

3 ways of improving memory:

a.

b.

c.

REVIEWING THE CONTENT

EXAMPLES

When people are giving lectures they often give examples to help their listeners understand better what it is they are talking about. Examples also help to make the idea being discussed more interesting and real. The speaker often gives a signal to show an example is going to be given. Some of these signals are listed below:

1. *Here's a good example of this.* Imagine that you are holding a lighted match . . .
2. *It's like* tossing a ball from one hand to the other . . .
3. *Let's try one more example.* Look at this sentence.
4. *For example,* do you remember what you ate for breakfast today?
5. *Let me give you an example.* When I was in junior high school, I had to . . .
6. *Say* you want to memorize the diameter of the Earth.

USING YOUR NOTES

Look back at your notes and give at least one example of the following terms to a partner. Your examples can be original examples, or you may use examples from the lecture.

1. short-term memory
2. long-term memory
3. recall
4. recognition
5. mnemonics
6. organization

PREPARING FOR THE TEST

In your next class, you will take a test on the content of this lecture. Before taking the test, answer the following questions.

1. Do you know the words in *italics*? Write a similar word or a brief definition.
   a. The *retina* of the eye is an important part of sensory memory.
   b. HOMES is a *mnemonic* used by some American high school students.
   c. Information in our brains is not *random;* it's well organized.

2. What are the three types of memory?
3. What are three ways of measuring memory?
4. What are three techniques for improving memory?

REVIEW: FINAL LISTENING

Now listen one last time to the lecture. Follow your notes as you listen.

TAKING THE TEST

Turn to page 100 and answer the questions. Do not use your notes.

PROJECTS

Try these projects after you have finished the Review Test.

1. Follow-up reading: Much has been written about memory — both research articles and articles on how to improve your memory. Locate a related reading. Report on it to the class.

2. Read this short article on a technique for learning vocabulary. After reading the article, tell your classmates about memory techniques you have used for learning English vocabulary.

EFFICIENT LEARNING

A German philosopher, Herman Ebbinghaus, began the scientific study of memory around 120 years ago. Ebbinghaus concentrated on studying how quickly the human mind can remember information. One result of his research is known as the **total time hypothesis.** This simply means that the amount you learn depends on the time you spend trying to learn it. In other words, our first rule of learning is this: If you study something longer, you tend to learn it more thoroughly.

Although it is usually true that studying for four hours is better than studying for one, there is still the question of how we should use the four hours. For example, is it better to study for four hours straight or to study for one hour a day for four days in a row? The answer, as you may have suspected, is that it is better to spread out the study times. This phenomenon, through which we can learn more efficiently by dividing our practice time, is known as the **distribution of practice effect.** Thus, our second rule of learning is this: It is better to study fairly briefly but often.

But we're not finished yet. We haven't considered how we should learn over very short amounts of time. Luckily, there is a very good answer, which is known as **micro-distribution practice.** Let's say you're trying to learn some new and rather difficult English vocabulary using flashcards. Should you look at the same word in rapid succession, or look at the word and then have some delay before you look at it again? The answer, which is our third rule of learning, is this: It is better to space out the presentations of the word.

To continue with our vocabulary card example, we can look at a technique created by Tom Landauer and Robert Bjork that works very nicely in the study of vocabulary. Essentially, we want to test a new item after a short delay and then, as the item becomes better learned, we should extend the delay. The idea is to test the item at the longest interval possible and yet get it right.

If a learner fails to remember an item, it should be presented after a shorter delay, and, whenever the learner is correct, the delay should be longer. One big advantage of this is that learners don't fail very often and so they don't get discouraged. Give this a try with a classmate or friend acting as the teacher before your next vocabulary test. You may find that it's better than the system you're using now!

THE FILMMAKING PROCESS

1 TOPIC PREVIEW

How can you experience the tension of being trapped in a submarine, the excitement of traveling through time, the terror of being chased by a criminal, or the joy of falling in love? It's simple — go to the movies! Through movies we can visit exotic places, meet beings from other worlds, watch unbelievable adventures, and, of course, learn about love! Whether it's laughter, tears, terror, or joy that you want to experience, the movies are a great place to find it.

WARM-UP DISCUSSION

In groups, discuss these topics with your classmates.

1. What kinds of movies do you like? What kinds do you dislike? Why?
2. What was the last movie you saw? Was it a horror film, a romance, or an adventure film?
3. List some steps that you think would be important in making a movie.
4. What do you think some of the most difficult or most expensive aspects of filmmaking might be?

VOCABULARY PREVIEW

Read the following sentences and try to guess the meaning of the words in *italics*.

1. Working on a script so that it's nearly perfect can be a very ***time-consuming*** process, often taking weeks or months.
2. ***Composing*** the music that will be part of the action of a film is a very challenging and exciting task for any musician.
3. The ***script***, which was about a hundred pages long, was written by a novelist.
4. The ***producer*** raised several million dollars for the movie in just three weeks. She asked many large companies to donate money for the film.
5. Alfred Hitchcock was a famous ***director*** who made numerous excellent films. Many famous actors and actresses were directed by him.
6. Actors and actresses have to memorize their ***dialogue*** before filming.
7. Many famous novelists do not want to sell their stories to filmmakers; like proud homeowners, they refuse to sell their ***property***!
8. The famous film *Casablanca* was filmed ***on location*** in Casablanca, Morocco.
9. Choosing the best scenes for a film is an ***enormous*** job. It's a lot of hard work for several people.
10. Making a full-length film is very ***complicated***. There are many difficult decisions to make.
11. The scene had to be reworked many times; ***editing*** each version was very time-consuming.
12. Filmmakers have many ***options*** in making a film; their decisions among these many options are very important in making a high-quality film.

Now fill in the blanks in the sentences below. Use the correct form of the words from above.

1. Actors and actresses do not always follow the original _____*script*_____ perfectly. They sometimes change the dialogue and actions while they are acting.

2. A movie can be filmed in a studio building or _____ in a real setting.

3. Actors have _____ jobs. They must remember many things at the same time — what to say, how to move, and so on. It's not at all simple.

4. The writer's book became a valuable _____ after it sold millions of copies.

5. Movies can be very _____ to make. Most take months and some more than a year.

6. _____ the songs for a musical is a very difficult job for the songwriter.

7. The director had two _____ to shoot the film in Mexico or Algeria. He decided on Mexico because the costs were lower there.

8. Many actors and actresses want to become _____ because they want to make films and also act in them.

9. The _____ had problems getting financial support for the movie.

10. Some stars have a difficult time memorizing the _____ for several scenes. Sometimes they must be told what to say.

11. The director made many changes to the movie while _____ it. He deleted some scenes and added new ones.

12. The movie required an _____ number of people — more than ten thousand.

WORD NETWORKS

These are some words and phrases you will hear in the lecture. Read the list. Ask about and discuss any words or phrases you do not know.

General terms
original story
intended
the very beginning
science fiction film
novels
musicals
original writer
specify
famous star
attract audiences
take attention away from
extensive
living accommodations
practical problems
satisfied
primary job
influence
impact
enhanced

Terms related to filmmaking
scriptwriter
camera shots
scenes
casting
filming
soundstages
indoor scenes
scenery
the best take
version
made its point
tempo
pace
sound track

Names
Back to the Future
The Sound of Music
Tess
The Godfather

Tom Cruise
Meryl Streep
Harrison Ford
E.T.

3 LISTENING TO THE LECTURE

BEFORE YOU LISTEN

You are going to listen to a lecture about the steps involved in filmmaking. Think about the process of making a film. List three steps you think are involved in making a movie.

1. _____

2. _____

3. _____

FIRST LISTENING: MAIN IDEAS

Listen to each part of the lecture to find out the main ideas. Circle a, b, or c.

PART 1

1. What is a property?
   a. a true story in a novel or magazine
   b. a story on which a movie is based
   c. a story written by a director

2. What step follows finding a property?
   a. finding the actors
   b. obtaining money
   c. writing a script

PART 2

1. According to the lecture, casting a movie is
   a. usually done in one of two ways.
   b. extremely important and always very expensive.
   c. done fairly quickly because of time pressure.

2. What step follows casting?
   a. filming
   b. choosing locations
   c. rewriting the script

PART 3

1. What are the final two steps mentioned in the lecture?
   a. recording the music and sending the film to theaters
   b. writing and recording the music
   c. editing the film and composing the music

SECOND LISTENING: FACTS AND DETAILS

Listen to each part of the lecture again. This time listen to learn more facts and details. Answer the questions below. Write T (true) or F (false) in front of each sentence.

PART 1

1. _____ The lecture deals with four basic steps in filmmaking.

2. _____ The most common type of property is an original story.

3. _____ The script only contains information about the dialogue.

PART 2

1. _____ It is always better to use famous actors than unknown actors.

2. _____ Scenes are always filmed in the same order in which they appear in the film.

3. _____ Filming usually takes place in two kinds of places: soundstages and real settings.

PART 3

1. _____ The film editor has a strong influence on the tempo of a film.

2. _____ The music is generally composed before filming is complete.

3. _____ *Cleopatra* was a very expensive movie to make.

4 TAKING NOTES

NUMBERING THE STEPS

Read the information below and discuss it with your classmates.

Probably the most basic and the most important purpose of taking notes is *organizing* the ideas in the lecture. In lectures that involve steps or stages, it is important to number the steps clearly. Usually, it is best to start each new step on the left-hand side of the page. This will help you when you review and discuss the ideas in the lecture.

Look at the following notes taken from Part 1 of the lecture. As you can see, these notes clearly number the steps or stages in filmmaking.

> How movies are made—6 major steps
> 1st step—find a property
>   * types of properties
>   1. an original story—e.g.,—Star Wars & Rocky
>   2. a property from a novel, play, or musical—e.g.,
>   The Godfather (novel)
> 2nd step—prepare the script
>   * the scriptwriter is sometimes the original writer

ORGANIZING YOUR NOTES

Now listen to the lecture again and take notes. Be careful to organize your notes by the steps or stages of the process.

REVIEWING THE CONTENT

P R O C E S S E S

One common pattern in lectures is the *process pattern*. Processes are related and dependent steps to reach a goal. Processes are used to give instructions and demonstrations (for example, in chemistry experiments) or in explanations of procedures to an audience (for example, how diamonds are mined or how films are made). When listening to a lecture that uses the process pattern, you can increase your understanding by remembering two points:

1. The steps in the process will have a logical, sensible order.

2. Each step will have a boundary. Often there will be a clear boundary marker between each step. Typical words and phrases that are often used to show step boundaries are:

First, second, third, etc.	*After that*	*Then*
To start with	*Once this is completed*	*The final or last step*
The first step	*Next*	*Finally*

USING YOUR NOTES

Look at your lecture notes. Explain the six major steps in the filmmaking process. Use some of the words and phrases from the list in the box above.

PREPARING FOR THE TEST

In your next class, you will take a test on the content of the lecture. Before taking the test, see if you can answer the following questions. Use your notes as you review.

1. Do you know the following terms? Write a similar word or a brief definition.
   - **a.** property
   - **b.** script
   - **c.** casting
   - **d.** filming
   - **e.** soundstages
   - **f.** on location
   - **g.** editing
   - **h.** composing

2. What are the two ways in which casting can be done?
3. What are the advantages and disadvantages of using "high-priced" (expensive) stars?
4. Filming can be done in two places. What are the advantages and disadvantages of filming on location?

REVIEW: FINAL LISTENING

Now listen one last time to the lecture. Follow your notes as you listen.

TAKING THE TEST

Turn to page 101 and answer the questions. Do *not* use your notes.

PROJECTS

Try these projects after you have finished the Review Test.

1. Write a review or give an oral report on a film you have seen recently.
2. Bring a recent newspaper to class. Look at the entertainment section. What movies are playing? Discuss which movies you would like to see and why.
3. Bring an ad for a movie to class. What information does the ad give you about
   a. who was involved in making the movie (who was the director, etc.)?
   b. how the movie was made (on location, using special effects, etc.)?
4. Work in groups of four to five people. Write or "re-create" a scene from a famous or popular movie. Don't worry about finding the script from the film; just use your memory of the film and your own words. Practice this scene a few times and then perform it for your classmates. Can they guess the film?

-VERBAL COMMUNICATION: YOUR BODY IS TALKING

1 TOPIC PREVIEW

All of us, at times, have trouble communicating with people. Sometimes we have difficulty communicating with people we've just met, and at other times we have problems communicating with people we know very well.

Sometimes our difficulties are caused by misunderstanding the words someone uses, but very often words are *not* the most important part of the conversation. On the contrary, some studies show that when expressing attitudes, 93 percent of the message is communicated by our tones of voice, our facial expressions, and our gestures. These things are known as non-verbal behavior. In other words, how we say things can be more important than what we say.

WARM-UP DISCUSSION

In groups, discuss these topics with your classmates.

1. Describe some common non-verbal behaviors and actions in your country.
2. What differences in non-verbal communication have you noticed between Americans and people from your country?
3. What are some differences between verbal and non-verbal communication?
4. Which is more "honest": verbal or non-verbal communication?

VOCABULARY PREVIEW

Read the following sentences and try to guess the meaning of the words in *italics*.

1. Americans point at their chests to indicate "me." This *gesture* seems strange to many Asians because they point at their noses.
2. My Italian friends use many different *facial expressions* when they talk. They often smile, look angry or surprised, and so on.
3. Margaret Mead was a famous *anthropologist* who went to Samoa to study the way of life of the people living there.
4. The word *run* has many meanings in English. Without some *context*, we don't know which meaning is being used.
5. My Japanese friend doesn't express negative *emotions* such as anger very much.
6. Happiness is a *universal* emotion. Everyone in the world expresses it the same way by laughing or smiling.
7. Because of movies and videos, American *culture* is well-known all over the world. Most people know how Americans will think or act in many situations.
8. This sentence is *ambiguous.* "I showed him an apple and an orange and he took it." *It* could mean the apple or the orange, so the meaning is not clear.
9. At first, I couldn't understand what the teacher said, but after her *clarification*, I could understand perfectly.
10. *Repetition* is important when learning. Doing something just once isn't enough.
11. John can't *conceal* his feelings. One look at his face and you know what he's thinking.
12. His *blushing* was surprising because he usually never gets embarrassed. His face was really red.

Now match each word with its correct definition.

1. ___j___ gesture
2. _____ facial expressions
3. _____ anthropologist
4. _____ context
5. _____ universal emotion
6. _____ emotions
7. _____ culture
8. _____ ambiguous
9. _____ clarification
10. _____ repetition
11. _____ conceal
12. _____ blushing

a. feelings such as joy or sadness
b. making clear or understandable
c. saying or doing something again
d. a person who studies people, especially their origins, classification, and social relationships
e. becoming red in the face because of shame, confusion, or embarrassment
f. aspects of a person's face that show emotion
g. having two or more meanings
h. a feeling expressed the same way in all cultures
i. hide something
j. a body movement that has some meaning
k. environment; parts of a situation that help us to understand the meaning of a word or action
l. beliefs and behavior of a group of people

W O R D   N E T W O R K S

These are some words and phrases you will hear in the lecture. Read the list.
Ask about and discuss any words or phrases you do not know.

Terms about communication
verbal comunication
aspect
encompasses
estimated
psychologists
meaning
behavior
determined
relationships
affection
comfortable
polite
feedback
situation
universal
vary
grammar
interact
dictionaries
sexual meaning
embarrasing
a huge mistake
recap

Non-verbal communication
kinesics
body movements
gaze
posture
speech rate
sweating
nervous
heartbeat

Names
Ray Birdwhistle
Richard Nixon

Gestures
frowns
smiles
raised eyebrows
shake hands
bow
hug

3 LISTENING TO THE LECTURE

BEFORE YOU LISTEN

This lecture is about non-verbal communication. Predict two of the ideas that the speaker might discuss in this lecture.

1. _____

2. _____

FIRST LISTENING: MAIN IDEAS

Listen to each part of the lecture to find out the main ideas. Circle a, b, or c.

PART 1

1. Non-verbal communication is
   a. less important than verbal communication.
   b. completely different from kinesics.
   c. concerned with such things as body movements and speech rate.

2. Raymond Birdwhistle was
   a. a famous American psychologist.
   b. the developer of the field of kinesics.
   c. the first person to compare cultures.

PART 2

1. The lecturer states that many people
   a. think that people from other cultures do not have non-verbal communication.
   b. believe all non-verbal communication is the same all over the world.
   c. believe non-verbal communication is more important than verbal communication in some cultures.

2. The lecturer also says that the system of non-verbal communication
   a. is well understood now by most anthropologists and psychologists.
   b. can be easily described by a "grammar" of non-verbal communication.
   c. changes so much from one culture to the next that it may never be understood.

PART 3

1. Clarification and repetition are
    a. often done with non-verbal communication.
    b. usually not possible with non-verbal communication.
    c. usually unnecessary with non-verbal communication.

2. Our verbal and non-verbal communication can be different because
    a. it's easier to conceal our true thoughts and feelings with non-verbal communication.
    b. the things we say and the things our bodies say are sometimes different.
    c. we can stop non-verbal communication more easily than we can stop verbal communication.

SECOND LISTENING: FACTS AND DETAILS

Listen to each part of the lecture again. This time listen to learn more facts and details. Answer the questions below. Write T (true) or F (false) in front of each sentence.

PART 1

1. _____ Kinesics is the study of speech rate, volume, and so forth.

2. _____ It is estimated that about 17 percent of our communication is non-verbal.

3. _____ Birdwhistle believed that non-verbal meaning depends on context.

PART 2

1. _____ Fear is a good example of a universal emotion.

2. _____ Non-verbal communication varies between cultures.

3. _____ The same non-verbal action may have different meanings in different situations.

PART 3

1. _____ It is easy to clarify and repeat non-verbal communication.

2. _____ Concealing our true feelings is often done non-verbally.

3. _____ In cases where verbal and non-verbal communication do not match, we usually believe the non-verbal information.

TAKING NOTES

USING ABBREVIATIONS

Read the information and discuss it with your classmates.

It's important to use abbreviations and symbols when we take notes in order to write efficiently and keep up with the lecturer. You are free to create your own abbreviations, but be very careful that you don't abbreviate too many words or abbreviate them too much. In many classes, you will often use your notes several weeks after you originally took them. This means that all of your abbreviations must be clear and easy to reconstruct. *Reconstruct* means "put back together."

Here are some common abbreviations:

e.g. = example (from Latin: *ex generalis*)   < = less than
etc. = and so on like this (from Latin: *et cetera*)   ∴ = therefore
+ or & = and   ] = includes
          = more than

You can also abbreviate long words and names by using the first syllable or initials:

kin = kinesics   R.B. = Raymond Birdwhistle
nvb = non-verbal behavior   com = communication
fb = feedback

The following notes are taken from Part 1. Can you reconstruct the notes, changing them into full sentences?

COMMUNICATION—most people think > v.com; talking
nonv com = more important
    orig → KINESICS — study of body move. in com.
        - body move → gestures, fac. exp., eyes, & post.
        - + sp. rate, vol.
R. B. - Am. anthro. "70% of com - nonv"
    - dev. "kinesics" — early 50's
    - "meaning of nvb depends on context"
        - e.g., a smile → many meanings

CHECKING YOUR NOTES

Now listen to the lecture again and take notes. Be sure to use abbreviations. When you finish, compare your notes with those of one or two of your classmates.

REVIEWING THE CONTENT

COMPARISON AND CONTRAST

Lectures are often concerned with comparing and contrasting two or more things. Important questions often considered in this pattern include:

1. How is one thing like another?
2. How is one thing different from another?
3. Is one thing better than another?

This pattern involves the use of particular words and phrases. Here are some examples of comparison and contrast in the lecture:

- In some cultures people shake hands, *whereas* in others people bow.

- *However,* there is another important aspect to communication.

- *In addition to* these things, we communicate with such things as our speech rate.

- The vocabulary of spoken language is somehow clear*er,* or at least easi*er* to write down, *than* that of non-verbal communication.

USING YOUR NOTES

Work with a classmate. Look at your notes and find three comparisons that were mentioned in the lecture.

PREPARING FOR THE TEST

In your next class, you will take a short test on the lecture. Before taking the test, be sure to review the following questions.

1. Do you know the following words? Can you use them in a sentence?
   a. non-verbal communication
   b. kinesics
   c. context
   d. universal emotions
   e. ambiguous
   f. clarification

2. Explain how verbal and non-verbal communication are different. Be sure to address the following points:
   a. naturalness and universality
   b. availability of formal definitions
   c. ability to conceal thoughts or feelings
   d. clarification and repetition

REVIEW: FINAL LISTENING

Now listen one last time to the lecture. Follow your notes as you listen.

TAKING THE TEST

Turn to page 102 and answer the questions. Do *not* use your notes.

6 PROJECTS

Try these projects after you have finished the Review Test.

1. Work in small groups and compare the following gestures with your classmates. Note how gestures can change from one country to the next. What gesture do you use in your country to express the following ideas?

    > Me.
    > Stop.
    > No.
    > Come here.
    > I'm full (after eating a big meal).
    > That person is crazy.
    > That's OK. / That's good.
    > I don't know.
    > I can't hear you.
    > Go away.

    Now show your classmates two more gestures from your country. See if they can guess what these gestures mean.

2. Telling the truth?
    Prepare a short autobiography (your own life story) to tell your classmates. However, when you tell your autobiography, you should make some of the important parts of your life story untrue! Your classmates will try to determine when you are lying, not only by your words, but also by your non-verbal communication — your tone of voice, facial expressions, the look in your eyes, and so on. Can you control your non-verbal behavior? How many times can your classmates tell when you are not telling the truth?

EFFECTS OF THE SUN

1 TOPIC PREVIEW

The sun provides us with life — the gifts of light and warmth that all animals and plants need to live and grow. Unfortunately, the sun can present us with dangers as well. Many of us do not understand the hidden dangers of the sun's rays and are unknowingly putting our health at risk by prolonged exposure to the sun. What is worse, the harmful side effects of exposure often may not show up until many years later.

WARM-UP DISCUSSION

In groups, discuss these topics with your classmates.

1. Do you enjoy sitting in the sun? Do you think you look better with a suntan? Do you feel better?
2. Have you ever gotten sunburned? How do you protect yourself against sunburn?
3. Do people in your country spend a lot of time in the sun?
4. In what ways do you think the sun can be dangerous?

VOCABULARY PREVIEW

Read the following sentences. Circle the letter of the word or phrase that is closest in meaning to the *italicized* expression.

1. ***Exposure*** to direct sunlight for long periods of time is very dangerous to our skin. We need to wear a shirt and a hat.
   a. being well protected
   b. making a lot of something
   c. being open to something
   d. being hot

2. The ***cancer*** started as a very small spot on his arm, but it spread quickly. Because of the danger, the doctor removed the spot.
   a. a disease in which cells grow uncontrollably
   b. a type of dark-colored hair
   c. a bruise
   d. a cut with a serious infection

3. ***Ultraviolet rays*** cannot be seen, but they can do great damage to our skin.
   a. a type of heat that we cannot feel
   b. a type of bright, red light
   c. a type of light invisible to the human eye
   d. a type of pain caused by the sun

4. ***Geography*** is an important factor in how people are affected by the sun. People from cold climates have less exposure to the sun.
   a. location; place
   b. time of day
   c. size of a family
   d. time of year

5. ***Environmental*** factors, such as the opportunities we have for different kinds of outdoor activities, can have an effect on our health.
   a. the conditions surrounding a person
   b. the cleanliness of the air
   c. the people we live with
   d. the amount of money we have

6. The sun is most direct in countries such as Colombia, Brazil, Zaire, and Kenya, which lie on the ***equator***.
   a. a place where there are jungles
   b. a type of large desert
   c. a place with very little rainfall
   d. the line midway between the North and South Poles

7. The ***ozone*** layer of the atmosphere is a natural barrier that stops some of the harmful sunlight from reaching the Earth; however, pollution is destroying ***ozone***.
   a. a type of industrial pollution
   b. a type of oxygen in the upper atmosphere
   c. thin, high clouds
   d. smoke in the atmosphere

8. Things like our hair and eye color are determined by ***hereditary*** factors. Children in the same family tend to have the same features.
   a. presents received from our parents
   b. training and education taught in schools
   c. characteristics passed from parents to their children
   d. items purchased by our parents

9. One of the **negative consequences** of staying in the hot sun for many hours can be very dry skin.
   a. extreme tiredness
   b. nicely tanned skin
   c. incorrect information
   d. bad results

10. People who rub **sunscreen** on their bodies before going out into the sun can often avoid skin damage.
    a. a large umbrella that blocks sunlight
    b. a special type of shirt that protects against the sun
    c. a lotion that protects against the harmful effects of the sun
    d. a large hat that keeps sunlight off of a person's face

11. **Caucasians** are more sensitive to the sun than darker skinned people.
    a. people who spend a great deal of time in the sun
    b. people who live in forests, jungles, and other shaded areas
    c. people who don't go outside very much
    d. fair-skinned people; for example, northern Europeans

12. Playing a lot of sports outdoors is a **behavioral** factor that can influence our health.
    a. the amount of exercise a person gets
    b. the ability to play a sport well
    c. the way a person lives and acts
    d. the hobbies a person has

WORD NETWORKS

These are some words and phrases you will hear in the lecture. Read the list. Ask about and discuss any words or phrases you do not know.

Medical terms
skin cancer
melanoma
genetic
SPF rating
sun protection factor
protective coating

Terms related to environment
direct sunlight
sun's rays
angle
atmosphere
radiation
filters out
UVA light
UVB light

General terms
potential cause
risk
at risk
lifestyle
outdoor jobs
scare tactic

Terms related to race
light-skinned (people)
light-eyed (people)
northern European background
Asians
Hispanics
blacks (Africans and others of African origin)

Names
American Cancer Society
"Fry Now, Pay Later"

3 LISTENING TO THE LECTURE

BEFORE YOU LISTEN

Look through the Word Networks list. Which of the words do you think are *technical words:* special words that will be explained during the lecture? Write them below.

_____   _____   _____

_____   _____   _____

_____   _____   _____

FIRST LISTENING: MAIN IDEAS

Listen to each part of the lecture to find out the main ideas. Circle a, b, or c.

PART 1

1. The main idea of Part 1 is that
   a. sunbathing is more dangerous than many people realize.
   b. there are various different reasons why people sunbathe.
   c. becoming well tanned is a major part of health and fitness.

PART 2

1. According to the lecture
   a. only hereditary factors influence the incidence of skin cancer.
   b. only environmental and behavioral factors influence the incidence of skin cancer.
   c. hereditary, environmental, and behavioral factors influence the incidence of skin cancer.

PART 3

1. One of the best ways to prevent sunburn is to
   a. use a sunscreen lotion.
   b. pay attention to anti-skin cancer campaigns.
   c. lie in the sun for less than two hours at a time.

2. UVA and UVB light are
   a. two chemicals found in many sunscreens.
   b. two types of ultraviolet rays.
   c. two types of skin cancer.

SECOND LISTENING: FACTS AND DETAILS

Listen to each part of the lecture again. This time listen to learn more facts and details. Answer the questions below. Write T (true) or F (false) in front of each sentence.

PART 1

1. _____ People have known how bad the sun is for the human body for hundreds of years.

2. _____ Fewer than 500,000 cases of skin cancer will be reported this year.

3. _____ Less than 19 percent of all skin cancer is directly related to exposure to the sun.

PART 2

1. _____ People of some races are more likely to get skin cancer than people of other races.

2. _____ Living near the equator will help prevent skin cancer.

3. _____ Severe sunburns during childhood can cause medical problems.

PART 3

1. _____ The "Fry Now, Pay Later" campaign by the American Cancer Society was successful.

2. _____ It's necessary to occasionally reapply sunscreen.

3. _____ Sensitive areas of the skin actually do not require sunscreen.

4 TAKING NOTES

USING SYMBOLS

Read the information below and discuss it with your classmates.

Symbols are abbreviations that show an idea or a relationship. Using symbols effectively can make taking notes much easier for you. By using symbols, you can keep up with the lecturer more easily.

There are hundreds of conventional, or fixed, symbols you can use. However, you can also develop your own set of "shorthand" symbols. The important thing is that *you* know what the symbols mean!

Here are some commonly used symbols:

=	is; equals	%	percent
≠	does not equal; is not the same as	+	and
+	to rise; to increase	...	continues
[	to go down; to decrease	→	leads to; causes
<	is less than; is smaller than	∧	part of; joined to
>	is more than; is larger than	*	see note below
$	dollars	∴	therefore; as a result

Look at the following notes from Part 1 of the lecture. How many symbols can you find?

Dangers of the sun
exposure to direct sun → cancer
this year > 600,000 cases of skin cancer
30,000 — melanoma*
6,500 deaths
90% of the cases ∧ exposure to the sun
*most serious type of skin cancer

USING SYMBOLS

Now listen to the lecture again and take notes. Be sure to use symbols. After you finish, look over your notes to find more places where you can use symbols instead of writing complete words, phrases, or sentences.

REVIEWING THE CONTENT

DESCRIPTION

Description is often an important part of lectures. In this unit, we heard the lecturer describe (1) the extent of the skin cancer problem today; (2) the type of person most likely to get skin cancer; and (3) the type of person who is well protected from the sun.

Description can include statistical information ("this year alone more than 600,000 cases will be reported . . . "), a list of factors ("in general, light-skinned, light-eyed people . . . are most likely to suffer from it . . . "), or a summary of actions ("a well-protected person will do several things — one, use a sunscreen . . . two, get a sunscreen that contains UVA . . . ").

USING YOUR NOTES

Look at your notes and describe the following three points to a partner:

1. the extent of the skin cancer problem
2. the type of person most likely to get skin cancer
3. a well-protected person

PREPARING FOR THE TEST

In your next class you will take a short test on the lecture. Before taking the test for this unit, see if you can answer the following questions.

1. Do you know the words in *italics?* Briefly define them.
   a. Skin cancer can be caused by too much *exposure* to the sun.
   b. *Ultraviolet* rays can damage our skin.
   c. It is clear that *geography* is an important factor in determining how likely we are to get skin cancer.
   d. The best defense against the sun is to use *sunscreen.*
   e. Getting severely sunburned at an early age can have *negative consequences* later on.

2. Name at least three factors that can increase a person's chances of getting skin cancer.
3. What are UVAs and UVBs?
4. How can we best protect ourselves against the damaging effects of the sun?

REVIEW: FINAL LISTENING

Now listen one last time to the lecture. Follow your notes as you listen.

TAKING THE TEST

Turn to page 103 and answer the questions. Do *not* use your notes.

6 PROJECTS

Try these projects after you have finished the Review Test.

1. Imagine that you are responsible for a campaign designed to promote the use of sunscreen lotion, particularly among teenagers on, say, the sunny coasts of Australia. Describe on paper, or orally, the main features of your campaign, and justify them—that is, say *why* they are a part of the campaign's design. Don't forget to include a slogan!

2. Find some articles in magazines or journals that deal with other growing health concerns (for example, the food we eat). Work in groups of three or four. Make an outline of your research and present your findings to the class.

3. Do a simple survey among your classmates. Find out what percentage of them use sunscreen lotion when they go out in the sun, what SPF rating they use, how many hours per week they are exposed to the sun, and how many severe sunburns they have had. Use the table below to record your data.

Name	Uses sunscreen? SPF rating?	Hours/week of exposure to sun?	Approximate # of severe sunburns?

MYSTICS AND PROPHETS

Nostradamus

1 TOPIC PREVIEW

Are you fascinated by the future? Most of us are. Fortune-tellers, seers, mystics, and horoscopes have existed for thousands of years. Some fortune-tellers have even changed history by influencing the decisions of great leaders. Even though we may not take fortune-tellers very seriously, we are intrigued by them nevertheless. Philosophers and scientists are also interested in the possibility of knowing and predicting the future.

WARM-UP DISCUSSION

In groups, discuss these topics with your classmates.

1. Do you believe it's possible to predict the future?
2. What are some methods that are used to predict the future?
3. Have you ever had your fortune told? Did you believe what the fortune-teller said?
4. Have you heard of Nostradamus? Do you know about any of his predictions?

2 VOCABULARY PREVIEW

Read the following sentences and try to guess the meaning of the words in *italics*.

1. *Prophets*, such as Muhammed, appear in history every 500 to 1000 years. They tell people about what will happen to the human race.
2. Some people's writings have to be *interpreted*. The meaning is not clear, so someone has to help readers decide what the writers meant.
3. Some people have *visions* in which they see angels or scenes from a future time.
4. *Mystics* believe they have some direct experience of God.
5. Our *imagination* gives us the ability to "see" the images described in books.
6. Some people claim they can make *predictions* about future events. They think they can tell what is going to happen.
7. Religious writings can be very *vague* at times. Their exact meaning is not clear.
8. Accurately predicting future events is *evidence* of a kind of mental power. If a person's predictions are usually accurate, we know they have a special ability.
9. *Astrologers* check the position of the stars in order to tell about a person's future.
10. Countries such as France and England have built great *empires* by controlling large parts of the world. The leaders of these countries tried to gain the land of other nations.
11. A terrible *disease* killed many people in Europe several hundred years ago. Many people got very sick and died.
12. San Francisco, being next to the Pacific Ocean, has a large natural *harbor*, where ships can come to shore.

Now fill in the blanks in the sentences below. Use the correct form of the words from above.

1. _____Astrologers_____ have been using the stars and planets to predict the future for an extremely long time.

2. Moses, who is considered to be a _____ by millions of people in the world, brought important social and religious laws to the Jewish people.

3. _____, deeply religious people who have spiritual experiences, can be found in almost every country.

4. Cities with excellent _____ tend to have a lot of ships coming and going.

5. This poem is too _____. I can't understand it well at all. It's not written very clearly.

6. The man said he had a _____ in which he saw an angel.

7. The ancient Romans built a great _____ and controlled much of Europe.

8. Prophecies are often _____ by different people in different ways because the meaning of the prophecy is usually not clear.

9. Nostradamus helped many sick people. This is _____ that he was a good man.

10. Children have good _____. They can believe they are cowboys, singers, or adults.

11. Doctors spend much time and energy trying to cure _____.

12. Some people make _____ about future events by using special cards.

W O R D   N E T W O R K S

These are some words and phrases you will hear in the lecture. Read the list. Ask about and discuss any words or phrases you do not know.

Terms related to prediction
divine prophet
horoscopes
negative predictions

Terms related to people
detached
selfish needs
spiritual union
higher power
direct knowledge
spiritual reality

General terms
warlike intent
medicine
fame
royalty
scourge

Names
Nostradamus
Montpellier
Paris
the plague
Middle Ages
Catherine de Medici
Prophecies
Centuries
Hiroshima
Nagasaki
Inland Sea
Pacific Ocean
Napoleon
Corsica

3 LISTENING TO THE LECTURE

BEFORE YOU LISTEN

Look at the Word Networks list. There are many proper nouns (the words beginning with capital letters). Although you do not need to be familiar with all of these proper nouns to understand the lecture, take some time to pronounce the names. This will help to prepare you for hearing them in the lecture.

FIRST LISTENING: MAIN IDEAS

Listen to each part of the lecture to find out the main ideas. Circle a, b, or c.

PART 1

1. According to the lecture
    a. Buddha and Muhammed are examples of mystics.
    b. Nostradamus was a divine prophet.
    c. there are two main kinds of prophets.

2. According to the lecture
    a. all mystics share some common traits.
    b. all mystics try to solve the world's problems.
    c. all mystics receive messages from mysterious voices.

PART 2

1. Nostradamus was considered by many people to be:
    a. a crazy person.
    b. a king.
    c. a hero.

Part 3

Paul Nay Loron ➤ Napaulon Roy

1. Nostradamus is most famous for
    a. his "negative predictions" of disasters and tragedies.
    b. causing disasters and tragedies.
    c. avoiding predictions of terrible events.

SECOND LISTENING: FACTS AND DETAILS

Listen to each part of the lecture again. This time listen to learn more facts and details. Answer the questions below. Write T (true) or F (false) in front of each sentence.

PART 1

1. _____ Divine prophets may also be called "religious prophets."

2. _____ Many mystics are very concerned about the problems in this world.

3. _____ Mystics sometimes need to make up new words to describe what they see.

PART 2

1. _____ Nostradamus lived in the 1500s.

2. _____ Nostradamus worked as a doctor and as an astrologer.

3. _____ Nostradamus was not well-known outside of France while he was alive.

4. _____ Nostradamus never wrote down his prophecies.

PART 3

1. _____ Nostradamus may have predicted the dropping of atomic bombs in World War II.

2. _____ Nostradamus predicted that Napoleon would save the French empire.

3. _____ Nostradamus made very few predictions other than the three explained in this lecture.

TAKING NOTES

Read the information below and discuss it with your classmates.

One student's notes for Part 1 of the lecture are shown below. As you can see, some of the words are underlined. These are key words and phrases in this section of the lecture.

Look at these notes carefully. Would you add to or delete anything from what is underlined here?

Nostradamus
Prophets—2 kinds
　1. divine prophet = religious proph. —interprets God's will
　　e.g., Buddha, Moses
　2. mystic—has visions, makes predictions
Mystics—3 things in common
　1. not concerned w. this world
　2. spiritual union w. God
　3. direct knowledge of spiritual reality (God)
　　Nostradamus—didn't have words to describe his
visions e.g., submarines

REVISING YOUR NOTES

Now listen to the lecture again and take notes. When you have finished, underline what you think are the key words and phrases. Then, work with a partner and compare the parts that you each underlined.

5 # REVIEWING THE CONTENT

DEFINITION

As we discussed earlier, words that have special or limited meanings are usually defined by the lecturer. The lecture in this unit includes a number of definitions.

Definitions are given in several ways:

1. Using an adjective clause: This is a kind of messenger *who* . . .
2. Giving types: We can classify prophets as *one of two types* . . .
3. Labeling: They are *what we might call* . . .
4. Giving a paraphrase: By spiritual reality *we mean* . . .
5. Making statements about the term: Horoscopes, as you probably know, give . . .

USING YOUR NOTES

Look at your notes and write definitions of the following words.

1. divine prophet
2. mystic
3. astrologer
4. horoscope
5. scourge
6. negative predictions

PREPARING FOR THE TEST

In your next class, you are going to take a short test on the lecture. Before taking the test, see if you can answer the following questions. Use your notes and talk with some of your classmates.

1. Do you know the words in *italics?* Briefly define them.
   a. Nostradamus was one of the most famous *mystics* to ever live.
   b. We must be very cautious when we *interpret* Nostradamus's writings.
   c. Some people consult an *astrologer* when they have to make an important decision.
   d. The plague was a *disease* that killed millions of people.
   e. Most of Nostradamus's writings are quite *vague.*

2. What kind of life did Nostradamus have?
3. The lecture discussed a few of Nostradamus's predictions. Name the topics that were covered and the basic predictions that he made.

REVIEW: FINAL LISTENING

Now listen one last time to the lecture. Follow your notes as you listen.

TAKING THE TEST

Turn to page 104 and answer the questions. Do *not* use your notes.

PROJECTS

Try these projects after you have finished the Review Test.

1. Supplementary reading: Have you read any recent articles or books about prophecies or predictions? If you have, please bring one to class and give a short summary of it.

2. Read this short article on Joan of Arc. Why was Joan of Arc killed? Do you know of any similar cases in which someone was persecuted because of unusual abilities, practices, or beliefs?

JOAN OF ARC

Nostradamus was not the only mystic to appear in the country of France. Born in 1412, nearly a hundred years before Nostradamus, was a simple peasant girl by the name of Jeanne d'Arc (in English, "Joan of Arc"). Although she was uneducated in the sense that she was never taught to read and write, her mother, a very sincere Christian, taught Joan all that she could about spiritual matters. As a result, Joan became known for her good character; she was said to be gentle, generous, and very spiritual.

Like many mystics before and after her, Joan had visions. Her visions, which she was certain were from beyond this world, convinced her that she had been chosen to help her country fight the English. At that time in history, France and England were fighting a war in which the French were doing quite badly. While only seventeen years old, Joan left her home and went to the town of Vaucouleurs and asked an army commander for a horse, some armor, and several men. Although the commander at first thought that she was surely insane, in the end he gave her what she asked for.

When the king of France, Charles VII, heard of the girl who was said to have been told by the saints of heaven that she should save France, he wanted to meet her. Rather than arranging a simple meeting, however, he decided to give a Joan a series of tests. The first test was that Charles had another man sit on his throne when Joan entered the room. When Joan walked in, she only looked at the man on the throne for a moment, and then she walked directly to the king, who was standing nearby. She had passed the first test by identifying Charles. Yet Charles was still not sure that Joan was a mystic, so next she told him what he had been thinking about during his private prayers. At this point, Charles believed in her. Ultimately, Joan was given a sword and command over the king's army.

The French military commanders soon discovered that when they followed her orders, they encountered nothing but success, and when they disobeyed her, they met with only defeat. Joan was not only a mystic, but also a military genius.

Joan fought and won numerous battles, but finally, in May of 1430, she was captured and put in prison by the British. The British said that Joan was a dangerous witch, but Joan insisted that the visions she had seen and the voices she had heard were divine messages.

On May 31, 1431, at the age of nineteen, the British prepared to kill Joan by burning her at the stake. She walked to her death with such courage that many people began to cry. One frightened Englishman turned away saying, "We are undone; we have burned a saint." When Joan was killed on that last day in May she passed into history to be remembered as one of France's greatest military commanders, a national heroine, and, as the Englishman had said, a saint.

THE BIOLOGICAL CLOCK

1 TOPIC PREVIEW

For centuries, people have dreamed of finding a "fountain of youth"— a magical formula that could stop the effects of aging. Today, no serious scientist hopes to find a magical formula to prevent aging, but biological scientists are getting closer to understanding why we age. They are also beginning to find ways to slow down the aging process. In fact, it's possible that at some point in the next century, 20 percent of the population could live into their nineties.

WARM-UP DISCUSSION

In groups, discuss these topics with your classmates.

1. How old is the oldest person you know? How long do you hope to live?
2. Do you think most people die of old age or of other causes?
3. How do people today try to stay young and live longer?
4. How might scientists go about extending human life? What kinds of medicines or treatments would be useful?

VOCABULARY PREVIEW

Read the following sentences and try to guess the meaning of the words in *italics*.

1. With the great-grandmother, grandmother, mother, and daughter all together, there were four *generations* in the same room.

2. Your eye and hair color are decided by the *genetic code* in your cells. This code contains information that you received from your parents' cells.

3. Science must break through many natural *barriers* if humans are to live more than 100 years. There are many problems and puzzles to be solved.

4. Our bodies contain many kinds of *cells* — for example, muscle, nerve, and blood *cells.* These are the smallest parts of our bodies.

5. Sickness *impairs* our ability to work hard. If we are sick, we are unable to use our bodies well.

6. We can live longer if we *eliminate* damaging foods and drinks from our diets. We should not eat or drink them if we wish to live as long as possible.

7. If the *immune system* is weakened, it cannot fight the viruses and bacteria that cause sickness. With a damaged *immune system*, a person gets sick very easily.

8. The *pituitary gland* is a small organ that controls several other glands, so it is often called the "master gland."

9. People without enough thyroid *hormones* can become very heavy even though they may not eat much at all. These *hormones* influence the digestion process.

10. Glands *secrete* hormones, which travel throughout our bodies. These secretions are very small amounts of liquid that enter our blood.

11. Without *oxygen* in the air for us to breathe, we could not live more than one minute.

12. The *nucleus* is at the center of each cell in the body. It is the most important part of a cell because it controls the life of the cell.

Now match each word with its correct definition.

1. ___l___ generations
2. _____ genetic code
3. _____ barriers
4. _____ cells
5. _____ impairs
6. _____ eliminate
7. _____ immune system
8. _____ pituitary gland
9. _____ hormones
10. _____ secrete
11. _____ oxygen
12. _____ nucleus

a. the smallest independent units in our bodies
b. a colorless, odorless gas necessary for life on Earth
c. a small gland attached to the brain that affects most basic bodily functions
d. produce and then give off
e. the information that determines heredity
f. things that limit movement or restrict entry
g. a part of the body that protects us from disease
h. get rid of; remove; delete
i. the central part of a cell
j. substances that influence body processes
k. damages
l. the periods of time between the birth of parents and their children

WORD NETWORKS

These are some words and phrases you will hear in the lecture. Read the list. Ask about and discuss any words or phrases you do not know.

Medical terms
aging process
Decreasing Consumption of Oxygen (DECO)
"death hormone"
brain
bodily functions
hearts
lungs
fighting infection
antidote
supply of cells

General terms
wear out
mechanical wear and tear
biological clock
influenced by
laboratory experiments
generations
overcome
moral
philosophical

Names
Dr. Leonard Hayflick
Stanford University

3 LISTENING TO THE LECTURE

BEFORE YOU LISTEN

Think about the question of aging. What do you think are the reasons that our bodies change as we age?

_____

_____

FIRST LISTENING: MAIN IDEAS

Listen to each part of the lecture to find out the main ideas. Circle a, b, or c.

PART 1

1. Which of the following was mentioned as the main reason for aging?
   a. Individual cells in our bodies harden and lose their flexibility.
   b. Our bodies simply wear out over time.
   c. Our bodies have built-in "clocks" that limit our life spans.

2. What is one of the effects of DECO?
   a. It increases the flow of blood in our bodies.
   b. It decreases the amount of oxygen in our system.
   c. It slows down the aging process.

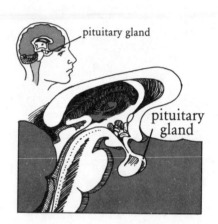

PART 2

1. What did Dr. Hayflick discover?
   a. Cells are regularly dying and being replaced.
   b. Cells can reproduce for approximately fifty generations.
   c. Cells don't always reproduce themselves perfectly.

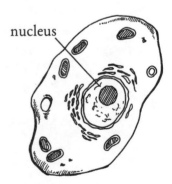

A typical human cell.

PART 3

1. The main issues concerning slowing down the aging process are
    a. basically medical issues to be decided by doctors.
    b. purely philosophical and moral questions.
    c. both scientific and philosophical problems.

SECOND LISTENING: FACTS AND DETAILS

Listen to each part of the lecture again. This time listen to learn more facts and details. Answer the questions below. Write T (true) or F (false) in front of each sentence.

PART 1

1. _____ The main secret to living longer is to exercise properly.

2. _____ DECO increases the number of hormones in our bodies.

3. _____ Our bodies produce more DECO as we become older.

PART 2

1. _____ There is a "program" in our cells that limits our life spans.

2. _____ Our genetic codes cannot control the number of generations for each cell.

3. _____ If an antidote to DECO could be found, people would stop aging.

PART 3

1. _____ All people will live to be 100 years old in the future.

2. _____ Scientists will probably find ways to extend our lives.

3. _____ The issues concerning slowing down the aging process will be easy to solve.

4 TAKING NOTES

USING SKETCHES

Read the information below and discuss it with your classmates.

Sometimes it is useful to include sketches in your notes. These will help you understand the material.

In this unit, it may be helpful to include rough sketches of the body, glands, and cells. Sketches help us to *visualize* ideas. *Visual ideas* are often very powerful and easy to remember.

MAKING YOUR NOTES MORE VISUAL

Now listen to the lecture again and take notes. Try to include some sketches in your notes.

REVIEWING THE CONTENT

CAUSE AND EFFECT

This lecture is concerned with cause-and-effect relationships. Remember that in these cases, we are concerned with the reasons and results of actions. By looking at your notes and thinking about the information in the lecture, you should be able to answer the following questions.

1. What are some causes of aging?
2. What are the consequences of DECO?
3. What would happen if the limitation Dr. Hayflick discovered could be overcome?

USING YOUR NOTES

Look at your notes. Can you label the parts below and fill in the blank spaces?

the _____ gland

This gland secretes

_____ .

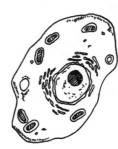

the _____

This contains the genetic

_____ .

A typical human

_____ .

PREPARING FOR THE TEST

In your next class, you will take a short test on the lecture. The test for this lecture will ask about the main ideas that were presented. Before taking the test, review your notes and discuss any questions you have with a small group of your classmates.

1. Do you know the following words? Briefly define them.

   a. barrier   **d.** hormone   **g.** cell
   b. DECO   **e.** immune system   **h.** oxygen
   c. secrete   **f.** pituitary gland   **i.** genetic code

2. What are two problems that scientists believe prevent us from staying young? Describe the principles involved. Check your notes.

REVIEW: FINAL LISTENING

Now listen one last time to the lecture. Follow your notes as you listen.

TAKING THE TEST

Turn to page 105 and answer the questions. Do *not* use your notes.

6 PROJECTS

Try these projects after you have finished the Review Test.

1. Bring to class at least two examples of newspaper or magazine advertisements that promote products that emphasize the importance of staying young. Present your examples to the class.

2. Suppose that in the next century the average life span increases to around 100 years of age. Working in a small group, list the positive and negative effects this might have on society. Present a summary of your lists to the class.

3. Should scientists manipulate the human body as described in the lecture? Is it all right for scientists and doctors to decide the future course of a person's life? Write a short essay explaining your views on this issue.

THE FIRST YEAR OF LIFE

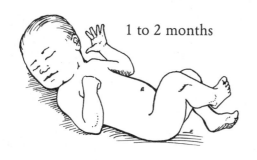

1 to 2 months

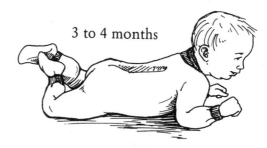

3 to 4 months

5 to 6 months

6 to 7 months

1 TOPIC PREVIEW

Birth is one of the miracles of life. However, to many parents, watching their babies' development take place in the weeks, months, and years after birth is a kind of second miracle. The development of young children has been studied a lot recently; as a result, many parents are trying to become better educated about the process of their babies' development. By understanding more about their children, mothers and fathers hope to be better parents.

WARM UP-DISCUSSION

In groups, discuss these topics with your classmates.

1. Do you like to be around young babies? Why or why not?
2. Do you think that babies develop quickly or slowly? Explain your answer.
3. What do you think a newborn baby can see and hear?
4. What does a baby learn during the first year of life?

VOCABULARY PREVIEW

Read the following sentences. Circle the letter of the phrase or expression that is closest in meaning to the *italicized* expression.

1. *Newborns* generally just drink milk for the first few months of their lives.
   a. babies
   b. teenagers
   c. middle-aged people
   d. old people

2. Babies *develop* rapidly. The rate at which they change is surprising to most parents.
   a. think; reason
   b. move
   c. evolve; grow
   d. learn to talk

3. *Gross movements*, such as large movements of the arms and legs, begin soon after birth.
   a. movements in which large body parts are used
   b. movements in which the fingers are used a lot
   c. movements in which the eyes are needed
   d. movements in which the fingers are important

4. It takes babies many months to begin using *delicate movements*, such as trying to hold an object.
   a. movements using the legs
   b. precise, skillful movements
   c. random, purposeless movements
   d. energetic, excited movements

5. Babies develop *motor skills*, such as crawling and walking in their first year.
   a. excellent vision
   b. the ability to swim
   c. movements using muscles
   d. the ability to communicate

6. Many babies say one-*syllable* sounds, such as "ma" and "ta" when they are a few months old.
   a. a long word
   b. a loud sound
   c. a kind of crying
   d. a simple unit of spoken language

7. The mother smiled when she heard her baby *coo.*
   a. make a soft, pleasant noise
   b. cry loudly
   c. say some simple words
   d. speak angrily

8. The baby tried to *focus on* Sara's face, but she was too far away. As a result, the baby couldn't see her well.
   a. to see something in a dark place
   b. to see something clearly
   c. to look for something that is lost
   d. to find something

9. Infants play with many *inanimate* objects such as toys and dolls. They're too young to play with pets or their brothers or sisters very much.
   a. not expensive
   b. easy to break
   c. large
   d. not living

10. Babies learn to *crawl* when they are about six months old. They can move quite quickly this way, but their hands and knees get very dirty.
    a. jump quickly
    b. walk by holding on to low furniture
    c. move along the floor using the hands and legs
    d. ride a small tricycle

11. Tiny babies can only say *vowel sounds* such as "ooh" or "aah."
    a. sounds in English usually spelled with *a, e, i, o,* or *u.*
    b. words that their parents understand
    c. sounds that have meaning
    d. sounds that babies make when they are unhappy

12. Babies who can say the *consonant sounds* "m" and "d," can say the words "mama" and "dada."
    a. words that have meaning to the mother and father only
    b. sounds that show non-verbal communication
    c. sounds that use the tongue, teeth, gums, or lips
    d. sounds that are made only for the baby

W O R D   N E T W O R K S

These are some words and phrases you will hear in the lecture. Read the list. Ask about and discuss any words or phrases you do not know.

Terms related to development
skill areas
physical development
language-interaction skills
patterns of development
responding
initiating an interaction

Physical movement
grasping
rolling over
picking up objects
turn their heads from side to side
eye movements
90 degrees

Interaction
social awareness
human touch
cuddling
follow an object
sociable
initiate
make silly faces
preferences
complaining
crying
fussing

Language
silly sounds
speech development
imitate
productive

3 LISTENING TO THE LECTURE

BEFORE YOU LISTEN

Think about some of the actions that babies learn to do when they are very young. List three of those actions here.

1._____

2._____

3._____

FIRST LISTENING: MAIN IDEAS

Listen to each part of the lecture to find out the main ideas. Circle a, b, or c.

PART 1

1. Part 1 of the lecture discusses
   a. what babies can do when they are one year old.
   b. how well babies can see, hear, and move.
   c. the general developmental pattern of babies.

PART 2

1. The lecturer talks about
   a. the development of newborns.
   b. the development of babies and young children.
   c. what parents can do to help their babies develop.

PART 3

1. Two-month-old babies are
   a. developmentally almost the same as newborns.
   b. slightly more developed than newborns.
   c. clearly more developed than newborns.

PART 4

1. A six-month-old infant can generally
   a. sit up and roll from front to back with help from an adult.
   b. sit up alone and crawl a little.
   c. sit up, crawl well, and walk a little.

SECOND LISTENING: FACTS AND DETAILS

Listen to each part of the lecture again. This time listen to learn more facts and details. Answer the questions below. Write T (true) or F (false) in front of each sentence.

PART 1

1. _____ We know about as much about the development of babies as we did twenty years ago.

2. _____ Gross motor movements generally precede delicate movements.

3. _____ Responses to language generally precede initiation of language.

PART 2

1. _____ Newborns can move their arms and legs in a limited way.

2. _____ Newborns can see clearly quite far from their faces.

3. _____ Newborns prefer to look at pictures of human faces.

PART 3

1. _____ Two-month-old babies cannot distinguish shapes and colors.

2. _____ Most babies begin to speak clearly around four months of age.

3. _____ Four-month-old babies are responsive to adults.

PART 4

1. _____ Most six-month-old babies are able to grasp objects in both hands.

2. _____ Many six-month-olds will respond when their names are called.

3. _____ Most six-month-old infants are comfortable with all people.

TAKING NOTES

MAKING A CHART

Read the information below and discuss it with your classmates.

Sometimes making a chart will help you to understand the information in a lecture. In this lecture, we hear how babies at four ages (newborn, two months, four months, and six months) are different. They are different in two skill areas (motor skills and language-interaction skills). Therefore, we can make a 4×2 chart to help us understand these differences.

	newborn (0–2 months)	2 months old	4 months old	6 months old
Motor Skills				
Language-Interaction Skills				

USING CHARTS IN YOUR NOTES

Now listen to the lecture again and take notes. Make a simple chart like the one above. Fill it in as you listen. You may also need to take other notes.

REVIEWING THE CONTENT

E X A M P L E S

In this unit's lecture, the speaker gives *examples* on several occasions to help clarify some points and to make the topic more real and interesting. The examples are introduced in various ways. Sometimes the speaker will mark the examples.
- *So, for instance,* a gross movement is . . .
- They make vowel sounds *like* "ooh" . . .

Most of the time, however, there is not a clear marker. The examples will simply follow the general statement.
- Newborns move their arms and legs in gross movements. . . . *They can also lift their heads and turn them* . . .
- Their language and social interaction are also developing. . . . *They respond when you talk to them* . . .

USING YOUR NOTES

Work with a classmate. Look at the lecture notes you have just completed and give examples of the following:

1. gross movements
2. delicate movements
3. what language skills a four-month-old has
4. what motor skills a six-month-old has

PREPARING FOR THE TEST

In your next class, you will take a short test on the lecture. Before taking the test, see if you can answer the following questions. Use your notes and talk in pairs or groups.

1. Do you know the words in *italics?* Briefly define them.
   a. *Gross movements* develop before *delicate movements.*
   b. *Motor skills* develop in a similar way in all infants.
   c. Many children learn to *crawl* around six months of age.
   d. Children *develop* in a predictable sequence.

2. Summarize the abilities of a newborn, two-month-old , four-month-old, and six-month-old baby.

REVIEW: FINAL LISTENING

Now listen one last time to the lecture. Follow your notes as you listen. Think about the examples given for each stage of a baby's development. If you still have any questions about the lecture, ask your teacher.

TAKING THE TEST

If you have reviewed the material, you should be ready to take the Review Test. Turn to page 106 and answer the questions. Do *not* use your notes.

6 PROJECTS

Try these projects after you have finished the Review Test.

1. Babies need a lot of things during their development. Listed below are some examples. In groups, rank them in order of importance and justify your order.
   a. physical activity
   b. close contact with loving parents
   c. pleasant physical environment
   d. music
   e. toys
   f. contact with other babies

2. What kind of special training for young children have you heard of? In small groups, make a list (of at least five kinds, if possible). What skills are being developed by these training programs? Do you think these programs are a good thing? Why or why not?

UNIT 11
Geology

THE DISAPPEARANCE OF THE DINOSAURS

1 TOPIC PREVIEW

Most of us know something about dinosaurs. Probably, this knowledge is the result of a fascination most of us had with them in our childhoods. Although it is certain that dinosaurs existed and reigned supreme on the Earth millions of years ago, it is still unclear why they suddenly vanished. Why did the dinosaurs disappear? This question has puzzled and challenged paleontologists (scientists who study ancient life forms) for years.

WARM-UP DISCUSSION

In groups, discuss these topics with your classmates.

1. When you were a child, were you interested in dinosaurs?
2. Have you ever seen a museum exhibit of dinosaurs? How did it impress you?
3. How do scientists learn about dinosaurs?
4. Do you know about how long ago the dinosaurs died out?

VOCABULARY PREVIEW

Read the following sentences and try to guess the meaning of the words in *italics*.

1. As the natural environment is being destroyed, more and more animals are becoming *extinct.* There are fewer and fewer of them alive.

2. Because he had studied *paleontology,* he was able to analyze and reconstruct the old bones and rocks and to date them.

3. Scientists have learned a lot about the Earth's past — and dinosaurs in particular — by collecting and analyzing *fossils,* which are set in rock.

4. The Earth's crust is composed of many *strata;* the deeper layers are the oldest.

5. There is more than one *theory* about the sudden disappearance of the dinosaurs. Scientists have developed some different ideas to explain what happened.

6. Animals that are not *adaptable* to changing environmental conditions die out.

7. An enormous, *cataclysmic* event must have occurred to kill off such a long-lasting, successful species as the dinosaurs.

8. Scientists can be alerted to a *meteor* in space that threatens or endangers the Earth, and missiles can be sent to reroute this dangerous rock to a safe path.

9. There is a 1 in 10,000 chance of a meteor's *colliding with* Earth in the next fifty years. Scientists want to prevent this kind of dangerous crash.

10. Scientific theories are generally thought to be unsatisfactory if there is no *evidence* to support them. Facts are necessary to support theories.

11. Meteors and asteroids travel so fast that if they hit the Earth, they would create a *basin* in the crust. Such a basin could be very deep.

12. Plants that receive sunlight are able to make certain chemicals through the process of *photosynthesis.*

Fill in the blanks in the sentences below. Use the correct form of words from above.

1. The archaeologists gave all the ___fossils___ they dug up to the museum.

2. The _____ sped toward the Earth at 65 kilometers (about 50 miles) per second.

3. Because dinosaurs died out millions of years ago, their bones cannot be found close to the Earth's surface, but in the lower _____.

4. Elephants, present-day creatures that remind us of the dinosaurs, are also in danger of becoming _____ due to the demand for their beautiful ivory tusks.

5. _____ is not possible unless plants get plenty of sunlight.

6. Many scientists believe that there isn't enough _____ to support a particular theory of why the dinosaurs died out.

7. Although there are many facts, there is no clear _____ to explain how this problem arose.

8. In 1989, an asteroid that was 250 meters (about 250 yards) wide came close —

   804,500 kilometers (about 500,000 miles), in fact — to _____

   _____ the Earth.

9. _____ is a fascinating study if you are interested in how life on Earth evolved, or developed.

10. Because of our intelligence, humans are a very _____ species; we are able to think of ways to adjust to changing conditions that might kill other living things.

11. The bottom of the _____ was 25 meters (about 25 yards) below the level of the surrounding land.

12. The earthquake was so _____ that it completely changed the look of the landscape so that it was unrecognizable.

WORD NETWORKS

These are some words and phrases you will hear in the lecture. Read the list. Ask about and discuss any words or phrases you do not know.

People
geologists
paleontologists
archaeologists

Words related to geology
rock formations
Earth's crust
volcanic activity
environmental conditions
meteor
crater
debris
atmosphere
finer particles
layer of dust
clay
fallout
striations
grooves
shock waves

Words related to theories
widely held theory
Climatic Changes Theory
Collision Theory
blocked out sunlight
Earth's temperature

Scientific terms
species
climatic changes
carbon dioxide
oxygen
iridium
quartz crystal

Names
Yucatán Peninsula
Cretaceous period
Tertiary period

3 LISTENING TO THE LECTURE

BEFORE YOU LISTEN

Think about the reasons that dinosaurs might have disappeared. Write one possible reason here.

FIRST LISTENING: MAIN IDEAS

Listen to each part of the lecture to find out the main ideas. Circle a, b, or c.

PART 1

1. The Climatic Changes Theory suggests that
   a. a lack of rain killed the dinosaurs.
   b. volcanoes changed the Earth's climate.
   c. extreme cold killed the dinosaurs.

PART 2

1. The new theory explaining why the dinosaurs disappeared, which is gaining increasing support, states that
   a. too little oxygen in the atmosphere was responsible.
   b. a meteor was responsible.
   c. the dinosaurs' inability to adapt was responsible.

PART 3

1. This part of the lecture discusses
   a. evidence for the meteor theory.
   b. the reasons why the meteor theory is inadequate.
   c. how iridium killed the dinosaurs.

SECOND LISTENING: FACTS AND DETAILS

Listen to each part of the lecture again. This time listen to learn more facts and details. Answer the questions below. Write T (true) or F (false) in front of each sentence.

PART 1

1. _____ Most people have little interest in dinosaurs.

2. _____ Dinosaurs died out about 6.5 million years ago.

3. _____ People from different fields of science have studied dinosaurs.

PART 2

1. _____ The Collision Theory suggests that 170 cubic kilometers (about 100 cubic miles) of debris may have been thrown into the atmosphere.

2. _____ Debris in the atmosphere would have greatly increased the rate of photosynthesis.

3. _____ The Collision Theory basically proposes that dinosaurs died from a lack of food.

PART 3

1. _____ There is a circular basin 1,100 meters (about 3,000 feet) below the Yucatán Peninsula.

2. _____ Rock of the Tertiary period has only a few dinosaur fossils in it.

3. _____ Quartz crystals from the Yucatán basin have marks that were caused by volcanic activity.

TAKING NOTES

WORKING WITH NUMBERS AND STATISTICS

Read the information below and discuss it with your classmates.

Whether you are studying social sciences or physical sciences, you will often work with numbers and statistics. In order to gain skills in hearing numbers correctly, you have to practice two things.

First, you need to discriminate between *stress markings,* since many numbers sound very similar except for stress differences.

Example: 13 — thir*teen*   30 — *thir*ty   19 — nine*teen*   90 — *nine*ty

Second, you need to listen carefully for *number group markers.* Numbers are given in groups of three digits, so for large numbers you must listen for markers of *millions, thousands,* and hundred/ten/single *units.*

Example: 25,678 — Twenty-five *thousand*//six hundred and seventy-eight
                          (*units*)//

             142,590 — One hundred and forty-two *thousand*//five hundred and
                          ninety (*units*)//

           4,064,150 — "Four *million,* sixty-four *thousand,* one hundred and fifty
                          (*units*)"

          18,244,876 — "Eighteen *million,* two hundred and forty-four *thousand,*
                          eight hundred and seventy-six (*units*)"

Stress and pause will usually help you identify these group markers.

For your reference, you should also note the expression of decimals (e.g., 2.41) and
        fractions (e.g., 2 2/5)

DECIMALS: 2.5 — two point five   0.02 — zero point zero two
FRACTIONS: 1/5 — one fifth 7/8 — seven eighths 2 1/3 — two and a third
   but . . .   1/2 — a half   1/4 — a quarter   1/3 — a third

INCLUDING NUMBERS IN YOUR NOTES

Now listen to the lecture again and take notes. Be careful to note down any important numbers that you hear. Of course, remember to take notes on *all* important aspects of the lecture and not *just* numbers.

REVIEWING THE CONTENT

SEQUENCES

The lecture in this unit describes the possible sequences of action that led to the extinction of the dinosaurs. However, as in many lectures, the speaker did not always use specific *time order* words and phrases to show the order of events. Often, when we listen, we must *think about the order* of events in order to understand the sequence.

USING YOUR NOTES

Look at your notes and write a short summary of how a meteor could have set off a process that may have led to the death of the dinosaurs.

PREPARING FOR THE TEST

In the next class, you will take a short test on the lecture. Before taking the test, see if you can answer the following questions. Use your notes and talk in pairs or groups.

1. Do you know the following words? Briefly define them.
    - **a.** extinct
    - **b.** paleontology
    - **c.** fossils
    - **d.** strata
    - **e.** meteor
    - **f.** striations
    - **g.** collide
    - **h.** adaptable
    - **i.** basin
    - **j.** debris
    - **k.** photosynthesis

2. What is puzzling about the disappearance of the dinosaurs?
3. How have we managed to increase our understanding of the dinosaurs? Who has done the research and what have they studied?
4. Can you summarize the Collision Theory? Think about why it is an attractive explanation.
5. What evidence is there to support the Collision Theory? Do you think it's adequate? Why or why not?

REVIEW: FINAL LISTENING

Now listen one last time to the lecture. Follow your notes as you listen. Think about the sequences of actions in the different theories. If you still have any questions about the lecture, ask your teacher.

TAKING THE TEST

If you have reviewed the material, you should be ready to take the Review Test. Turn to page 107 and answer the questions. Do *not* use your notes.

6 PROJECTS

Try these projects after you have finished the Review Test.

1. Supplementary report: Go to the library. Locate at least one resource book on dinosaurs, or use an encyclopedia article on the subject of dinosaurs. Report on one aspect of dinosaurs that was not dealt with in this lecture.

2. Supplementary reading: Read this short article on fossils, then summarize it to one of your classmates.

EFFICIENT LEARNING FOSSILS: A CLUE TO THE EARTH'S PAST

The most common animal fossils are shells, many of which are microscopic, one-celled animals called foraminifers. They are often found in oil deposits and can thus help in the search for oil. Larger shells, such as those of snails, are also common, as are the hard parts of corals and sea lilies (which are animals) and lamp shells, which are often preserved in rocks without chemical change.

However, major changes have often taken place in the shells. Water containing minerals has often seeped through the rocks and ultimately changed all the substances that composed the shell when the animal was alive, even though the shell may still have kept its exact, original form.

Frequently, the buried shell fossil is dissolved by groundwater and only a cavity is left in the rock, which preserves the shape of the fossil. This cavity is, in effect, a mold that can be filled by paleontologists to get an accurate plaster cast of the original fossil.

Bones and teeth are also common animal fossils and may be preserved without much change, except that organic material decays, leaving only the hard, mineral substance of the bone itself. Usually, the spaces left empty by decay become filled with some other mineral such as lime or silica. The bone becomes harder and heavier and feels like stone, although it has not really turned to stone; the original hard, bony substance is still there and the only important change is that something has been added. Teeth are usually preserved with even less change because they are harder than bone to begin with and contain fewer microscopic spaces.

Fossil plants may be preserved as imprints — leaves are particularly common. These may simply be molds left after the surrounding rock has hardened and the actual leaves have decayed and disappeared. Often, however, some of the original substance of the leaves remains in the form of a brown or black film of carbon.

An interesting type of plant fossil is called petrified wood. In this case, a part of the tree is buried in the ground. Water then fills in the porous spaces in the wood with mineral matter.

There are various other types of fossils — fossil footprints and trails, for example. If an animal walked or crawled over soft mud or sand and this was covered by another layer of sediment before the trail had disappeared, the track may be preserved after the whole deposit has hardened into rock. Dinosaur tracks of this kind have been found in the Connecticut Valley and have given us information about dinosaurs whose bones are unknown.

Finally, eggs are one especially rare type of fossil. Some famous dinosaur eggs were found in the Gobi Desert, for example. Today, such eggs can collect high prices.

FASHION IN THE TWENTY-FIRST CENTURY

1 TOPIC PREVIEW

Have you ever stopped to think how much our daily lives are influenced by fashion? People will often make judgments about the kind of people we are based on the kinds of clothes we wear and the types of cars we drive. This is perhaps truest of all in the case of clothing and the way we dress. Clothing speaks louder than almost anything else, and fashion designers know this only too well.

WARM-UP DISCUSSION

In groups, discuss these topics with your classmates.

1. What kinds of clothes do you like to wear?
2. What types of clothes and colors for clothing are now popular in your country?
3. How do you think technology might influence fashion?
4. What do you imagine clothing fashions will be like ten or twenty years from now?

VOCABULARY PREVIEW

Read the following sentences and try to guess the meaning of the words in *italics*.

1. As times change, political and *social trends* also change. People's ideas are always changing.
2. Clothing designers make many *practical* clothes that can be worn every day.
3. If you live in a very cold or very hot climate, *functional* clothes are more important than stylish ones. People care more about comfort than style.
4. As technology improves, methods of designing are becoming more and more *sophisticated.* Advanced designs can even be computer-generated in some cases.
5. *Fabrics* such as silk and cotton are often used in the clothing industry.
6. Along with what we say and do, the clothes we wear are one of our best means of *personal expression.*
7. If you are an important person who attends many business and social functions, it is important to understand *dress codes.* You don't want to be out of place because of what you are wearing.
8. Older people tend to have more *conservative* ideas and opinions about dress than young people. Their ideas and opinions don't change very quickly.
9. Some companies have many *restrictions* on the clothes employees can wear. For example, short skirts or shorts are sometimes prohibited.
10. Many Americans like to wear *informal* clothes like jeans because they are comfortable.
11. Some clothing manufacturers have *computerized* factories, so they need fewer workers. Their computers can often do the planning and design work better than people.
12. Many people think that *disposable* goods are convenient because they do not need to be cleaned or repaired. People throw them away when they are old and buy new ones.

Now match each word with its correct definition.

1. ___c___ social trends
2. _____ practical
3. _____ functional
4. _____ sophisticated
5. _____ fabrics
6. _____ personal expression
7. _____ dress codes
8. _____ conservative
9. _____ restrictions
10. _____ informal
11. _____ computerized
12. _____ disposable

a. showing one's personality
b. using a computer to do some task
c. tendencies in a society or social group
d. useful
e. relaxed style
f. limitations
g. advanced; highly developed
h. practical; has a purpose
i. can be thrown away
j. rules about how to dress
k. traditional; not progressive
l. the materials clothing is made with

WORD NETWORKS

These are some words and phrases you will hear in the lecture. Read the list.
Ask about and discuss any words or phrases you do not know.

General terms
distant future
technology
cycles
science
powerful influence

Terms about fashion
clothing industry
fashionable
classical
fashion designers
formal
decoration
traditional
sportswear
pastel-colored
sex specific
cosmetics
fabric selection
tailors
seamstresses
natural materials
engineered fabrics
artificial

New ideas about fashion
solar belt packs
body paints
surroundings
decor
body temperature
"in thing"
programmed
gluing
fusing

3 LISTENING TO THE LECTURE

BEFORE YOU LISTEN

Think about the following questions: What kind of clothes do you think you'll be wearing twenty years from now? How will they be different from the clothes you're wearing today?

Your answer:

_____

FIRST LISTENING: MAIN IDEAS

Listen to each part of the lecture to find out the main ideas. Circle a, b, or c.

PART 1

1. The lecturer states that
   a. it is impossible to predict future fashions.
   b. it is possible to accurately predict future fashions.
   c. predicting future fashions is difficult, but intelligent guessing is possible.

PART 2

1. At the beginning of the twenty-first century
   a. clothes will be more functional.
   b. dark colors will increase in popularity.
   c. clothes will be simpler and more colorful.

2. In 2010 clothes will be:
   a. practical and a means of personal expression.
   b. fashionable and sophisticated.
   c. simple but luxurious.

PART 3

1. According to this part of the lecture
   a. men's clothes will become more casual and sportier.
   b. three piece suits will disappear.
   c. men's makeup will disappear.

2. The lecturer states that women's business clothes will
   a. use mostly expensive fabrics like linen.
   b. become quite conservative.
   c. use many soft, pretty colors.

PART 4

1. Which of the following is not true?
    a. "Disposable" clothes will grow in popularity.
    b. Computers will be used more in clothing design.
    c. Clothes will be generally more expensive.

SECOND LISTENING: FACTS AND DETAILS

Listen to each part of the lecture again. This time listen to learn more facts and details. Answer the questions below. Write T (true) or F (false) in front of each sentence.

PART 1

1. _____ Technology influences fashion.

2. _____ Understanding social trends is little help in predicting future fashion trends.

3. _____ Classical styles never become unfashionable.

PART 2

1. _____ We may be able to adjust the temperature of some clothes in the future.

2. _____ Body paints would serve both a practical and cosmetic purpose.

3. _____ Future clothes may be sensitive to the wearer's emotional states.

PART 3

1. _____ Men will wear pastel-colored clothes more often in the future.

2. _____ Men's clothing will become more like women's fashions.

3. _____ Dress codes will probably be more restrictive in the future.

PART 4

1. _____ There will be an increasing need for tailors and seamstresses.

2. _____ Natural animal furs will not be used at all.

3. _____ Jeans represent a certain kind of social attitude.

TAKING NOTES

A REVIEW OF NOTE-TAKING TECHNIQUES

Read the information below and discuss it with your classmates.

Let's review some of the note-taking techniques that successful note takers use:

1. formatting notes — main ideas and supporting facts
2. using abbreviations and symbols
3. noting key words and phrases
4. listing and enumerating
5. using sketches
6. working with charts
7. noting statistics and numbers

Do you use these techniques when you take notes? What other helpful techniques do you use?

REVIEWING NOTE-TAKING TECHNIQUES

Now listen to the lecture again and take notes. Use the techniques listed above. When you have finished, work with a partner or in a small group and compare your notes. Fill in any important information you did not note during the lecture.

REVIEWING THE CONTENT

COMPARISON AND CONTRAST

The lecture in this unit is concerned with *describing* future fashions. An important type of description is the comparison of two ideas or things. In this lecture, the speaker compares current fashions with future fashions. There are many expressions that are used in comparing items. Here are some common ones.

COMPARISON — to show similarities		CONTRAST — to show differences	
likewise	both . . . and . . .	but	on the other hand
in a similar manner	as . . . as	while	different from
similarly	like	however	rather than
not only . . . but also	similar to	unlike	conversely

USING YOUR NOTES

Work with a partner and, using the information in your notes, compare at least three of the following:

1. men's business clothes of today versus men's business clothes of the future
2. women's business clothes of today versus women's business clothes of the future
3. ways of making clothes today versus ways of making clothes in the future
4. fabrics used today versus fabrics of the future
5. technological features of clothing today versus in the future

PREPARING FOR THE TEST

In your next class, you will take a short test on the lecture. Before taking the test, be sure to review the following questions.

1. Do you know the words in *italics?* Briefly define them.
    a. *Fabrics* such as silk are very popular.
    b. *Functional* clothes are important in very hot or very cold places.
    c. Business clothes tend to be quite *conservative.*
    d. The cost of *disposable* clothing would probably be low.

2. What are some of the predictions for the year 2010?
3. What are some ways in which technology will influence fashion?

REVIEW: FINAL LISTENING

Now listen one last time to the lecture. Follow your notes as you listen.

TAKING THE TEST

Turn to page 108 and answer the questions. Do *not* use your notes.

6 PROJECTS

Try these projects after you have finished the Review Test.

1. Give a three-minute presentation on this topic: "The movement for sexual equality has an effect on fashion."
2. Imagine clothing styles in the years 2050 to 2100. Design one article of clothing and explain its design and function.
3. The use of cosmetics by men is increasing. What do you think about this trend?
4. "Trying to keep up with the latest fashions is a waste of money." Write an essay agreeing or disagreeing with this statement.

UNIT 1 Review Test

Answer each question in the space provided.

1. When did the first comic strip appear in a U.S. newspaper?

2. What are the topics in satirical comics?

3. What is one main feature of the characters in adventure comics (e.g., *Dick Tracy* or *Superman*)?

4. Describe a typical dramatic comic strip.

5. Why do you think people read the comics section of a newspaper?

UNIT 2 Review Test

Answer each question in the space provided.

1. What is the definition of advertising?

2. What is the difference between factual and emotional appeals in advertising?

3. Which of the three advertising techniques discussed in the lecture do you think is the most effective? Why do you think it is better than the others?

4. Do you think it is right for rock stars to advertise products? Support your opinion.

UNIT 3 Review Test

Answer each question in the space provided.

1. What kinds of companies and organizations are popular targets for hackers?

2. What comments did the film *War Games* make about hacking?

3. What are the three common motivations of people who engage in hacking and computer crime?

4. What was the near tragedy that involved the Memorial Sloan-Kettering Cancer Center's computer system?

5. What is being done to control computer crime?

6. What do you think is the best way to stop computer crime? Support your answer.

UNIT 4 Review Test

Answer each question in the space provided.

1. What is sensory memory? How can the length of sensory memory be discovered?

2. What are some differences between short- and long-term memory?

3. Explain why recognition is usually easier than recall.

4. Describe one technique for improving memory. Give an example of how it works.

UNIT 5 Review Test

Answer each question in the space provided.

1. Describe the first stage of filmmaking.

2. What is the main job of a scriptwriter?

3. *E.T.* was mentioned as an example of a movie that employed what kind of actors and actresses?

4. What are two advantages of using unknown actors and actresses in a movie?

5. About how long does it usually take to film a movie?

6. What are some concerns in editing a movie?

7. When is the music for a movie usually recorded?

8. What was the most expensive movie ever made (using a 1992 dollar conversion)?

UNIT 6 Review Test

Answer each question in the space provided.

1. What is kinesics?

2. Raymond Birdwhistle said that the meaning of non-verbal behavior, such as a smile, depends on the context. Explain briefly what he meant by this.

3. What are universal emotions? Give two examples.

4. Give one example of how non-verbal communication can differ from one culture to another.

5. List three ways in which verbal and non-verbal communication differ.

6. What is one idea from this lecture that is of most interest to you? Why?

UNIT 7 Review Test

Answer each question in the space provided.

1. What type of people are most likely to get skin cancer?

2. How is geography related to skin cancer?

3. Why should parents be especially careful about their children's exposure to the sun?

4. Explain what an SPF rating is.

5. What tips would you give to someone who wants to know how to best use sunscreen?

6. What do you consider to be the main point of this lecture?

UNIT 8 Review Test

Answer each question in the space provided.

1. How are a divine prophet and a mystic different?

2. Name two things that mystics have in common.

3. Briefly describe Nostradamus's life.

4. Choose one of these topics: Napoleon or Hiroshima and Nagasaki. What predictions did Nostradamus make?

UNIT 9 Review Test

Answer each question in the space provided.

1. What is the name of the hormone scientists call the "death hormone," and how does it cause our bodies to age?

2. At about what age does the body start producing this hormone?

3. What gland produces this hormone?

4. What seems to be the limit to our supply of cells?

5. Where do the "instructions" for the number of generations for a cell come from?

6. Do you think it is a good thing that scientists are learning how to slow down the aging process? Explain your reasons.

UNIT 10 Review Test

Answer each question in the space provided.

1. Describe the general developmental pattern of infants. (Use the terms *from . . . to.*)

2. Describe some of the main developments of motor skills in infants from newborns to two, four, and six months of age.

3. What are some indications that infants are naturally interested in forming social relationships with others?

4. How does a child's language develop in the first six months of life?

UNIT 11 Review Test

Answer each question in the space provided.

1. How long ago did the dinosaurs die out?

2. What is the Climatic Changes Theory?

3. Why do many scientists believe that climatic changes did not cause the extinction of the dinosaurs?

4. How does the Collision Theory explain the suddenness with which the dinosaurs disappeared from the earth?

5. Describe one piece of evidence that supports the Collision Theory.

UNIT 12 Review Test

Answer each question in the space provided.

1. How might men's clothes in the future differ from those of today?

2. Describe two changes in clothing that may occur as a result of advanced technology.

3. Do you agree that technology will have a strong impact on future fashions? Give reasons for your position.

4. In your opinion, why do people follow fashions?

UNIT 1

VOCABULARY PREVIEW

2. b 3. a 4. c 5. d 6. a
7. c 8. d 9. c 10. c 11. a 12. c

LISTENING TO THE LECTURE

First Listening: Main Ideas	Second Listening: Facts and Details
PART 1	PART 1
1. b	1. False
	2. False
	3. True
PART 2	PART 2
1. b	1. True
	2. True
	3. False
PART 3	PART 3
1. a	1. False
	2. False
	3. False

UNIT 1 Review Test

1. The first comic strip appeared in 1895.

2. The topics in satirical comics are actually rather serious. Some examples might include politics or the idea of justice in society.

3. Characters in adventure comics tend to be clearly divided between those who are good and those who are evil.

4. A dramatic comic strip is drawn rather realistically and the plot resembles a TV soap opera. Romance and human relationships are the primary topics.

5. (possible answer) I think people read the comics section of the newspaper for entertainment. I also think they like to identify with the extreme situation of the characters. Some comics, such as adventure comics, are exciting, and people like to feel some excitement or adventure in their lives.

UNIT 2

VOCABULARY PREVIEW

2. sponsors 3. target 4. focus on 5. prestige
6. are influenced by 7. techniques 8. promote 9. convincing
10. consumers 11. reinforce 12. major distinction

LISTENING TO THE LECTURE

First Listening: Main Ideas	Second Listening: Facts and Details
PART 1	PART 1
1. b	1. False
	2. False
	3. False
PART 2	PART 2
1. c	1. True
2. b	2. False
	3. True
PART 3	PART 3
1. a	1. True
2. b	2. True
	3. True

UNIT 2 Review Test

1. Advertising is the transmission of a message designed to promote a product, service, or idea.

2. Factual appeals are directed toward our intellect. That is, they provide information regarding how a product works, some special features of that product, or reasons why we should buy the product. They hope to convince us through persuasive facts. Emotional appeals, on the other hand, focus on our needs for love and prestige, or our desire to be attractive. As the name says, they focus on bringing out human emotions.

3. (possible answer) Testimonials are possibly the most effective. It's difficult to write a truly good slogan, and repetition, although important, is not enough by itself. If a person that we respect or like advertises a product, we will be sure to pay attention to the ad. In addition, our opinion of the product's value or quality will become more favorable.

4. (possible answer) Yes, it is acceptable for rock stars to advertise products. They have a right to earn a living in any (legal) manner they see fit. It is important, however, that they control certain artistic aspects of the advertising. Their songs should not be presented in a way that they dislike. The integrity of the song must not be lost.

UNIT 3

VOCABULARY PREVIEW

2. b   3. d   4. l   5. g   6. h
7. k   8. j   9. f   10. c   11. e   12. a

LISTENING TO THE LECTURE

First Listening: Main Ideas	Second Listening: Facts and Details
PART 1	PART 1
1. b	1. True
	2. True
	3. True
PART 2	PART 2
1. c	1. False
2. a	2. False
	3. False
PART 3	PART 3
1. a	1. True
	2. True
	3. False

UNIT 3 Review Test

1. Financial institutions, such as banks and insurance companies, are the main targets of hackers.

2. The film *War Games* pointed out that computer crime is a real problem in modern society and that it's tempting to some people because it's challenging and possibly rewarding.

3. The three common motivations for hacking are: (1) financial gain; (2) malice; and (3) the challenge of breaking into a computer system.

4. A hacker broke into the hospital's computer and erased some files. That computer monitored medical equipment and also contained patients' medical records. If the hacker had damaged, destroyed, or altered those files, a tragedy might have occurred.

5. Courts are being tougher and computer security is improving. For example, less obvious passwords are being used, and access-control software and "dial back" systems have been developed. Scrambling devices and audit trails are also available.

6. (possible answer) Some people will always be trying to break into computers unless they know it's just not possible. Developing more effective ways of protecting computer systems from hackers is the best way to stop computer crime.

UNIT 4

VOCABULARY PREVIEW

2. b   3. b   4. b   5. a   6. a
7. a   8. d   9. c   10. c   11. c   12. d

LISTENING TO THE LECTURE

First Listening: Main Ideas	Second Listening: Facts and Details
PART 1	PART 1
1. b	1. True
2. a	2. True
	3. False
PART 2	PART 2
1. c	1. True
2. c	2. False
	3. True
PART 3	PART 3
1. a	1. True
2. b	2. False
	3. False
PART 4	PART 4
1. c	1. True
2. a	2. False
	3. False

UNIT 4 Review Test

1. Sensory memory is the memory that we have when something makes an impression on one of our senses—sight, hearing, et cetera. Sensory memory lasts for only a brief moment. Waving a match in a dark place and noticing how long it takes for the image to fade is a way of measuring visual sensory memory.

2. Some differences between short- and long-term memory include:
   • The length of the memory—Short-term memory lasts for as long as we focus on the item, whereas long-term memory can last our whole lives.

   • Short-term memory is necessary for tasks such as calculation and reading, whereas long-term memory is not as involved in these processes.

   • Long-term memory is focused on meaning, not exact words, whereas short-term memory recalls information in a detailed manner.

3. Recognition is easier than recall because when we use recall, we have no clues or hints. We must ask ourselves, "What did I see?" whereas in recognition, we are choosing from a list and asking ourselves, "Have I seen this before?"

4. (possible answer) One technique for improving memory is to personalize information. For example, if I'm in a history class and I need to remember the date 1844, I might think that when I was 18 years old, my father was 44 years old. This information, because it's related to my life, is easy to remember.

UNIT 5

VOCABULARY PREVIEW

2. on location 3. complicated 4. property
5. time-consuming 6. composing 7. options 8. director
9. producer 10. dialogue 11. editing 12. enormous

LISTENING TO THE LECTURE

First Listening: Main Ideas	Second Listening: Facts and Details
PART 1	PART 1
1. b	1. False
2. c	2. False
	3. False
PART 2	PART 2
1. a	1. False
2. a	2. False
	3. True
PART 3	PART 3
1. c	1. True
	2. False
	3. True

UNIT 5 Review Test

1. The first stage of filmmaking is to find a property, which is the story the film will be based on. There are two kinds of properties: an original story that has never appeared before or a story that was first presented as a book, a musical, or a play.

2. The scriptwriter writes the dialogue and specifies the camera shots that should be used.

3. *E.T.* is an example of a hit movie that didn't use any big stars. The actors and actresses were chosen because they fit the parts well, not because of their fame.

4. The first advantage is that using relatively unknown performers is much cheaper than using big stars. In addition, unknown actors and actresses don't take attention away from the story like a big star might.

5. Most major motion pictures take six to eight months to film.

6. Some important points in editing a movie are: (1) selecting the best take; (2) knowing when to move on to the next scene and; (3) maintaining an appropriate tempo.

7. The music is usually recorded after the movie has been made. The conductor actually watches the film while recording the music.

8. *Cleopatra* was the most expensive movie ever made. It cost (in 1992 dollars) $194 million.

UNIT 6

VOCABULARY PREVIEW

2. f 3. d 4. k 5. h 6. a
7. l 8. g 9. b 10. c 11. i 12. e

LISTENING TO THE LECTURE

First Listening: Main Ideas	Second Listening: Facts and Details
PART 1	PART 1
1. c	1. False
2. b	2. False
	3. True
PART 2	PART 2
1. b	1. True
2. c	2. True
	3. True
PART 3	PART 3
1. b	1. False
2. b	2. False
	3. True

UNIT 6 Review Test

1. Kinesics is the scientific study of body movements used in communication.

2. This means that the same behavior can have a different meaning depending on the situation. For instance, smiling at a person you've just met can be a way of showing friendliness. However, if a child who has just been punished by a parent smiles, it may be a way of showing defiance.

3. Universal emotions are emotions that are communicated non-verbally the same way throughout the world. One example is fear, in which a person's eyes and mouth open widely. Other universal emotions include joy, sadness, and anger.

4. Sometimes the same gesture can have various meanings depending on the culture. The example given in the lecture was the "OK" symbol, which has different meanings in North America, South America, and Japan.

5. 1) We have dictionaries to explain the meaning of words (verbal communication), but none to explain the meaning of non-verbal communication in a particular culture.
2) Although we can ask someone to repeat or clarify verbal communication, it's difficult or impossible to do with non-verbal communication.
3) Non-verbal communication is more honest than verbal communication. It's harder to lie using non-verbal communication.

6. (possible answer) I'm interested in the idea that the same behavior can have different meanings depending on the situation or the culture. This makes non-verbal communication a very complex and therefore interesting area to study.

UNIT 7

VOCABULARY PREVIEW
2. a 3. c 4. a 5. a 6. d
7. b 8. c 9. d 10. c 11. d 12. c

LISTENING TO THE LECTURE

First Listening:
Main Ideas

Second Listening:
Facts and Details

PART 1
1. a

PART 1
1. False
2. False
3. False

PART 2
1. c

PART 2
1. True
2. False
3. True

PART 3
1. a
2. b

PART 3
1. True
2. True
3. False

UNIT 7 Review Test

1. People with light skin and light-colored eyes who have a northern European background are the most likely to get skin cancer.

2. The farther north or south of the equator you are, the less likely you are to get skin cancer. This is related to the directness of the sun's rays.

3. Getting sunburned badly and/or frequently while a person is young can make that person more likely to get skin cancer when he or she becomes older. For this reason, it is important to protect young children from the sun.

4. *SPF* means "sun protection factor." A sunscreen with a sun protection factor of 15 will protect you from sunburn fifteen times longer than normal. For example, what if you were in a very hot place where you might begin to burn in fifteen minutes? By wearing SPF 15 sunscreen, you could stay in the sun 15 x 15 minutes (225 minutes) before you would start to burn.

5. When using a sunscreen, it's important to (1) put on the sun screen fifteen to thirty minutes before going into the sun; (2) reapply it once every two hours or more often if you are swimming or exercising and; (3) put plenty of sunscreen on sensitive areas such as the ears, neck, and nose.

6. (possible answer) The main point of the lecture is that skin cancer is a real danger for many people in the world, but that some people are more likely to get the disease than others. The final point was that we can protect ourselves, primarily by using sunscreen properly.

UNIT 8

VOCABULARY PREVIEW
2. prophet 3. mystics 4. harbors 5. vague 6. vision
7. empire 8. interpreted 9. evidence 10. imaginations
11. disease 12. predictions

LISTENING TO THE LECTURE

First Listening:
Main Ideas

Second Listening:
Facts and Details

PART 1
1. c
2. a

PART 1
1. True
2. False
3. True

PART 2
1. c

PART 2
1. True
2. True
3. False
4. False

PART 3
1. a

PART 3
1. True
2. False
3. False

UNIT 8 Review Test

1. A divine prophet delivers a divine message to humankind and communicates God's will. Some examples are Buddha, Jesus Christ, and Muhammed. A mystic does none of these things, but is a person who has visions and makes predictions about the future.

2. First, mystics are often not directly concerned with the problems of this world. Second, they often claim to experience a kind of spiritual union with a higher power.

3. Nostradamus studied medicine at Montpellier, which was a very good university at that time. He became a doctor and helped many people who had the plague, a terrible disease that killed millions in Europe. In addition, he was a famous astrologer who made horoscopes for royalty. Late in life, he began having his visions and he wrote two famous books about those visions— *Prophecies* and *Centuries*.

4. (possible answer) Nostradamus spoke of an emperor who would be born near Italy and who would "cost the empire dearly." In reality, Napoleon was born near Italy in Corsica, and, through his leadership, France was nearly destroyed.
(possible answer) Nostradamus predicted that in two cities near a harbor "two scourges" would happen—that is, something would cause great suffering in these two places. He also said there would be hunger and disease. These predictions are accurate if we think about Hiroshima and Nagasaki, which were struck by atomic bombs.

UNIT 9

VOCABULARY PREVIEW
2. e   3. f   4. a   5. k   6. h
7. g   8. c   9. j   10. d   11. b   12. i

LISTENING TO THE LECTURE

First Listening: Main Ideas	Second Listening: Facts and Details
PART 1	PART 1
1. c	1. False
2. b	2. False
	3. True
PART 2	PART 2
1. b	1. True
	2. False
	3. False
PART 3	PART 3
1. c	1. False
	2. True
	3. False

UNIT 9 Review Test

1. DECO is the name of the "death hormone." DECO weakens our bodies by decreasing the supply of oxygen in our bodies. Less oxygen impairs many bodily functions.

2. The body begins producing DECO around the age of twenty.

3. DECO is produced by the pituitary gland.

4. According to Dr. Leonard Hayflick, the limit for most cells is approximately fifty generations.

5. The "instructions" are found in the genetic code of the cell, which is in the cell's nucleus.

6. (possible answer) Although human beings have a natural desire to live as long as possible, it might be a bad idea to try to extend our life spans. First, overpopulation is already a terrible problem in many parts of the world. Second, perhaps only rich or privileged people would be able to get the treatments necessary to extend their lives. This would cause greater injustice in our world.

UNIT 10

VOCABULARY PREVIEW
2. c   3. a   4. b   5. c   6. d
7. a   8. b   9. d   10. c   11. a   12. c

LISTENING TO THE LECTURE

First Listening: Main Ideas	Second Listening: Facts and Details
PART 1	PART 1
1. c	1. False
	2. True
	3. True
PART 2	PART 2
1. a	1. True
	2. False
	3. False
PART 3	PART 3
1. c	1. False
	2. False
	3. True
PART 4	PART 4
1. b	1. True
	2. True
	3. False

UNIT 10 Review Test

1. In terms of motor skills, babies develop from gross movements to delicate ones. Language and interaction skills develop from responding to language to initiating interaction.

2. As newborns, babies can make gross movements with their arms and legs, and lift their heads and turn them. At two months, they are able to push their heads and chests up, follow an object 90 degrees, and bring their hands together. By four months of age, they can roll over from their backs to their fronts and vice versa, stand with help, grab and hold on to things, and follow objects 180 degrees. When they are six months old, they can sit up alone, put all of their weight on their legs, possibly crawl a little bit, hold something in each hand, and move things from hand to hand.

3. We can understand that infants are interested in forming social relationships with others because they (1) prefer to look at real human faces rather than pictures; (2) respond positively to human touch by cuddling; (3) smile purposefully at others and initiate smiling, and; (4) show excitement and happiness when they see someone they know or like.

4. At first, children respond to voices, especially their mothers'. Next, they begin to produce sounds, beginning with single-syllable vowel sounds followed by two-syllable vowel sounds. After this, they begin to produce consonant sounds.

UNIT 11

VOCABULARY PREVIEW

2. meteor   3. strata   4. extinct   5. photosynthesis   6. evidence
7. theory   8. colliding with   9. paleontology   10. adaptable
11. basin   12. cataclysmic

LISTENING TO THE LECTURE

First Listening: Main Ideas	Second Listening: Facts and Details
PART 1	PART 1
1. b	1. False
	2. False
	3. True
PART 2	PART 2
1. b	1. False
	2. False
	3. True
PART 3	PART 3
1. a	1. True
	2. False
	3. False

UNIT 11 Review Test

1. Dinosaurs died out approximately 65 million years ago.

2. The Climatic Changes Theory tries to explain why the dinosaurs died suddenly. It says that volcanoes threw large amounts of dust into the atmosphere—so much that the earth's climate changed. As a result of these changes, the dinosaurs died.

3. Many scientists doubt the Climatic Changes Theory because it doesn't explain the speed at which the dinosaurs died out. The dinosaurs had adapted extremely well for millions of years, so scientists don't believe that volcanoes could have changed the climate so completely and rapidly that the dinosaurs would have died suddenly.

4. The Collision Theory says that a large meteor hit the Earth and threw extremely large amounts of debris into the air. This debris may have blocked the sunlight immediately and for a matter of months. This would have killed plants quickly, which would have killed the dinosaurs. In this scenario, everything would have been normal one day, and a few months later, most of the plants and dinosaur life would have disappeared.

5. (possible answer) One simple piece of evidence that supports the Collision Theory is the discovery of a circular basin 180 kilometers (about 113 miles) in diameter in the Yucatán Peninsula. This basin, which is 1,100 meters (3,000 feet) underground, was formed around the time of the disappearance of the dinosaurs. This could be a crater caused by a large meteor striking the earth.

UNIT 12

VOCABULARY PREVIEW

2. d   3. h   4. g   5. l   6. a
7. j   8. k   9. f   10. e   11. b   12. i

LISTENING TO THE LECTURE

First Listening: Main Ideas	Second Listening: Facts and Details
PART 1	PART 1
1. c	1. True
	2. False
	3. False
PART 2	PART 2
1. a	1. True
2. a	2. True
	3. True
PART 3	PART 3
1. a	1. True
2. b	2. True
	3. False
PART 4	PART 4
1. c	1. False
	2. False
	3. True

UNIT 12 Review Test

1. In the future, men's clothes might change in several ways. First, traditional clothing might be replaced with sportswear and very relaxed styles. Second, pastel colors may be much more popular and the clothing may become generally looser.

2. Solar belt packs would allow the wearer to adjust the amount of solar energy that would come through the fabric. Body paints would allow the wearer to paint on underwear to protect his or her body from the cold.

3. (possible answer) I agree that technology will have an impact on future fashions. I believe there will be new types of fabrics and ways of producing clothing in the future because of technology. These changes may inspire designers to do new things. Additionally, people who work outdoors may be able to wear completely different types of clothing than what is worn now. For example, heavy clothing worn in the winter may no longer be necessary. Changes in society and a greater mixing of cultures in the future will also give designers many new ideas.

4. (possible answer) People follow fashions for several reasons. One reason is in order to be socially acceptable to a certain group of people. For example, people in business have to dress in a similar way to their peers. Another reason is that some people copy others that they admire. For instance, if a popular movie star wears up-to-date fashions, it will influence some people to do the same. A third reason is simply because people like "new looks" in modern fashion.

UNIT 1 The World of Comics

Narrator: This is the kind of lecture you would hear in a journalism class. This lecture concerns a common form of mass media—newspapers—and, in particular, one section of the newspaper.

PART 1

Hello, everyone. We'll continue our discussion of American newspapers today. Does anyone care to guess what the most popular section of the paper is? Well, it's not the front page, the weather report, or even, sorry to disappoint you sports fans . . . it's not the sports column. It's the comics. Now, my bet is that even those of you who rarely read the paper at all can't resist glancing at the comics. True?

Well, today, since it is important for journalists and for journalism students to understand the comics section, not just to enjoy it, I'll tell you a little more about several types of comics that can usually be found in American newspapers. There are hundreds . . . actually . . . thousands of papers all across the country that have comics sections. As a matter of fact, in the entire country, only two major newspapers don't have comics sections. One is the *New York Times* and the other is the *Wall Street Journal*. This shows you just how widespread comics are.

Actually, the first comic strip to become fairly popular in the U.S. appeared in a New York newspaper in the year 1895. The comic strip was called ***Hogan's Alley***. It was so popular with the readers that newspapers all across the country began printing comics of their own. The **primary** purpose of *Hogan's Alley* was **entertainment**, or we might say humorous entertainment. Not surprisingly, comics of this type are called **humorous comics.** Of course, many modern comics fit into this category. A well-known example in the United States, and even many other countries today, is something like ***Peanuts*** with its chief characters **Snoopy** and **Charlie Brown.**

Humorous comics are often simply drawn and not very **realistic** in terms of how they're drawn. Actually, many **characters** in these comics—such as Charlie Brown—are very **un**realistic . . . they don't look like real people at all. Not only are the drawings—and the **backgrounds**—simple, but they are usually **funny-looking**. The reader is already smiling and amused even before reading what the characters have to say. Children who are too young to read show us this by looking at and laughing at these comics.

So what are the themes in these humorous comics? Just **everyday things** . . . everyday things like eating breakfast,

commuting to work, talking to the boss, or watching television are the common topics for humorous comics. These common activities become funny because of the silly and **unexpected things** that the characters say. Many readers **identify with** these characters because they have been in similar circumstances. In addition, impossible things are often possible in humorous comics. For example, dogs can talk or at least think like humans, as Snoopy does, and people can fly.

Narrator: Stop the tape and answer the questions for Part 1. . . . Now, let's continue with the lecture. The lecturer will discuss two more types of comics.

PART 2

By the 1920s, comics had progressed to the point that they began to combine both humorous and serious **topics**. These comics, which we call **satirical comics**, make **humorous comments** about serious situations. OK, let me repeat that: Satirical comics make humorous comments about serious situations. For example, ***Little Orphan Annie***, which appeared in 1924—I'm sure many of you have never seen this comic—but, anyway, it managed to be humorous and at the same time express the serious **political views** of the writer, which were that the poor people in America were living difficult lives that were very different from those of the rich. This was a comic picture of the **political injustice** of the 1920s.

Of course, several modern comics are of this type, notably ***Doonesbury*** and ***Bloom County***. These frequently make profound comments regarding well-known American politicians and political situations. They make us laugh, particularly if we know something about American **politics**, but at the same time they force us to think about various political situations. For instance, during the 1991 Gulf War, the comic strip *Doonesbury* made some serious comments about the war, while still entertaining the readers.

Satirical comics are similar in many ways to humorous comics. Drawings are often very simple and characters are also funny-looking. The difference lies in the conversations that the characters have. The first type, humorous comics, are just funny, whereas satirical comics try to make a serious point using humor and **sarcasm**. Topics are different, too: They might include politics, the environment, or **current trends** in society. Obviously, the audience of satirical comics will differ somewhat from that of humorous comics. Some people just want to be entertained and don't want to think about important social issues when they read the comics.

The third major type of comics is **adventure comics**. These began to appear about a decade later . . . in the 1930s. Most of you should be familiar with the character Dick Tracy because of the 1990 movie. He was originally in a typical adventure comic of the same name. *Dick Tracy* first appeared in, let's see, . . . 1931, around the same time as another extremely well-known adventure comic—*Superman*. As with the previous two types of comic strips, adventure comics can easily be found nowadays in newspapers, and they usually have a large **audience**. Lots of people like to read adventure comics.

Adventure comics—both the characters and the backgrounds—tend to be drawn more realistically. They are drawn in some detail. If you compare them with, say, humorous comics, it is quite easy to see the difference. The **plots** are different too in the sense that they generally revolve around danger and **violence**. Also—and this is a big difference—the main characters in adventure comics tend to be either clearly good or clearly evil, and the action is the fight between these two forces. Violence is very common in this type of comic.

Narrator: Stop the tape and answer the questions for Part 2. . . . Now, let's continue with Part 3. In this section, the lecturer will discuss the last type of comics.

PART 3

All right, our fourth type, and the last type that we will discuss is **dramatic comics**. These are very similar to many TV **soap operas**—the kind of dramas you can see on afternoon television. I'm sure you know what I mean. What are the themes of dramatic comics? As I am sure you figured out, they tell about **romance** and **human relationships**. The themes of this type of comic are events in the lives of ordinary people. *Mary Worth* is a well-known dramatic comic. The main character, Mary Worth, is a kind and wise older woman who gives advice to her younger friends. And the pictures—this means both the characters and the background—are drawn quite realistically. Of all the types of comics we've talked about so far, dramatic comics are by far the most realistic.

Today, comics have started to take a different turn, but these four types—humorous comics, satirical comics, adventure comics, and dramatic comics—are both the history, and I predict, the future of comics in newspapers . . . and are likely to be an integral part, and perhaps the most popular part of newspapers for a long time to come.

Narrator: Stop the tape and answer the questions for Part 3.

UNIT 2   The Keys to Advertising

Narrator: This is the kind of lecture you would hear in a mass media course. This particular lecture looks at three different advertising techniques.

PART 1

Today's topic is advertising—what it is and why it is effective. . . . First, I'll explain the field of advertising in general terms, and then I'll talk about different types of **appeals** used in advertising, and finally I'll discuss some specific **techniques** that are used in advertisements.

Well, just what is advertising? I think we would all agree that advertising is basically a kind of message or **message transmission** . . . that is designed to **promote** a product, service, or even an idea. Let's repeat that: Advertising is a kind of message transmission that is designed to promote a product, promote a service, or promote an idea. Got it? Advertising, my friends, is a big money industry. In fact, just in the United States alone, advertisers pay a total of $90 billion a year to have their messages transmitted . . . and, because advertising is so large and so **pervasive**, it really has a powerful effect on all facets of American society. Advertising influences us in every way . . . from the products that we buy to the way that we think about issues.

Advertising reaches us in many ways. This is one reason behind the powerful influence of advertising . . . it comes in so many forms . . . in **printed form**—that is, in newspapers and magazines—or in **audio form**—over the radio—and also in **audiovisual form** —on television. Printed . . . audio . . . and audiovisual. . . . Advertisements bombard us with their messages in all of these **media**. No one can fully escape their effect.

So, just how does advertising work? Well, advertising has to do two things in order to be successful. First, the advertisement must be interesting enough to **attract the customer's attention**; that's absolutely essential. Sounds simple, doesn't it? In reality though, because of the vast amounts of advertising that flood the media today, this is an extremely difficult task. It takes some very creative thinking to design a truly interesting ad.

Second, even if an advertisement manages to catch our attention, it then has to give us some very **convincing** reasons for believing its message and buying the product. The key word here is *convincing*—the audience must receive a clear reason why they need the product that is being advertised. This is achieved by using a variety of techniques.

Narrator: Stop the tape and answer the questions for Part 1. . . . Now listen to Part 2 of the lecture in which some general comments about advertising techniques are made and one type of appeal is discussed.

PART 2

OK, let's take a look at some of the common advertising techniques employed in the media today. . . .

Uh, I think, first of all, that the basis of all techniques is appeal, a-p-p-e-a-l. Appeal is the **main selling point** or theme of the ad. Now, there are fundamentally two kinds of appeals: the **factual appeal** and the **emotional appeal**. Let's look at factual appeals first. A factual appeal tells how a product is made or how it works. The goal of the advertisement is to impart some useful information about the product . . . what it is, how it is made, or how it works. The advertisement should leave us with the idea that it has been "proven" that this product is superior. Information is the important point here. What about the emotional appeal? An emotional appeal **focuses on** how a product will give us **personal satisfaction**. Emotional appeals try to influence us by exploiting our human needs for love and **prestige**, or our desires to be **socially acceptable** and **personally attractive**. The promise is that the product will make us more likable. OK, that's the **major distinction**—factual appeals provide information and emotional appeals promise personal satisfaction.

Now let's look at a concrete example. Keeping in mind the definitions of factual and emotional appeals, what kind of appeal do you think ads with big stars, say **Michael Jackson**, in them will usually use? Well, as I'm sure you guessed, they use emotional appeal. They tell us that if we use their product, we'll be just as popular and sexy as Michael Jackson, or that Michael Jackson will like us for using this product. That, friends, is emotional appeal.

Now, a kind of appeal is not all that is necessary for a successful ad. Advertisements must employ some techniques to ensure that this appeal is effectively communicated to the intended audience.

The first technique that I'd like to explain is the use of **slogans**. A slogan is a short phrase that an advertiser uses over and over in its ads. Slogans are usually short and easy to remember. The British shoemaker, **Reebok**, is a good example of a company that has a short and very effective slogan. Back in 1988, I think it was, and some of you might remember this, Reebok sponsored a major **Amnesty**

International tour featuring such stars as **Bruce Springsteen**, **Tracy Chapman**, and **Sting**. Oh, by the way, for those of you who don't know, Amnesty International is a worldwide organization that is actively trying to ensure that people's rights and freedoms are protected.

Anyway, Reebok's slogan was "**Reeboks let U.B.U.**" Let U-B-U . . . just using the letters U, B, U. . . . Reebok's slogan was trying to say that by wearing their shoes, "You can just be yourself." It was a short slogan, unique, easy to remember, and it was a fitting slogan for a tour that was helping ensure the freedom of people around the world. I'm sure all of you can think of other slogans that advertisers use. How about the slogan, "Don't leave home without it." That slogan will be associated with American Express for a long time to come.

Narrator: Stop the tape and answer the questions for Part 2. . . . Next, in Part 3 of the lecture, two more techniques are discussed.

PART 3

Well, let's move on to the next technique . . . **testimonials**. Testimonials are advertisements that have people—sometimes famous, sometimes not—tell us that they use and like a certain product, and that we will like it too! They may say this very directly, or they may just imply it by, say, taking a big spoonful of a breakfast cereal and smiling. . . . Those of us watching will assume that they love the cereal!

Most people **are influenced by** what others say, especially if the person saying it is someone famous or someone whom we admire. Rock star testimonials are a very effective way to influence young people to buy a certain product. They're their heroes, so what they say must be true! We all want to be just like our heroes!

An example of one of the most famous testimonials in recent times involves Michael Jackson. In the 1980s **Pepsi** hired Jackson for their ads. At that time he was very popular . . . he was a hot property, having just had a lot of hit songs in a row . . . he actually rewrote his hit song "**Billy Jean**" for the commercial. Having Michael Jackson and his song "Billy Jean" so closely connected with Pepsi made for a very powerful advertisement and the obvious message was "Michael Jackson drinks Pepsi and you should too."

Pepsi used testimonials in another way, too, at about the same time. In order to **target** a specific ethnic group, young **Hispanics**, the Pepsi Cola Company sponsored a tour by **Gloria Estefan and Miami Sound Machine**, a band made up of Hispanic musicians. Being the **sponsor** ensured that Pepsi's ads were seen and heard at the concerts, on the radio, and in music stores . . . whenever the concerts themselves were advertised. The people who were interested in the concert naturally associated Pepsi and Gloria Estefan. Again, a very effective use of an implied testimonial.

Let's see, we've looked at the techniques of slogans and testimonials . . . and now I'd like to mention one last technique before I stop today . . . **repetition**. As the name suggests, repetition means to run an ad again and again. Repeated impact . . . a company's **promotional idea** can be built or **reinforced** quickly by using this technique. Most advertisers believe that the more often people see or hear an ad, the more they'll want the product. Pretty simple thinking, but it seems to work. Repetition is important for ensuring that an ad will be remembered.

Singer **Whitney Houston** selling **Diet Coke** illustrates this technique perfectly. Her ads were posted everywhere, in newspapers and magazines, on posters and billboards. And when the ads ran on TV, they unfailingly ran two or three times in a row. This repetition had an **incredible effect** on the popularity of the product. . . .

Well, I'll wrap things up by saying that I certainly hope you realize that advertising is a serious business, and that certain appeals and techniques in advertising are used to convince people to buy certain products, services, and ideas. . . . It is important for us, as **consumers**, to be aware of these appeals and techniques, and it's also important, if you go into the advertising field, to use these appeals and techniques fairly and honestly.

Narrator: Stop the tape and answer the questions for Part 3.

UNIT 3 Computer Crime

Narrator: This is the kind of lecture you might hear in a computer science course. The lecturer looks in particular at the problem of computer crime, the kinds of problems computer hacking can cause, and ways of increasing computer security.

PART 1

All right, why don't we get started here. . . . How many of you own and can operate a computer? . . . two, four, six, . . . let's see . . . nineteen; hmm, that's quite a few of you. OK well, we all know how popular . . . no, not just popular . . . how necessary business and family computers are becoming and how much a part of modern-day life they are now; and so today, I am going to talk about computers. But actually, I don't intend to talk about the function and operation of computers, but about a problem that is both worrying and very **dangerous:** computer **crime**. Let's look more closely at this modern crime.

One thing is certain: Computers and specifically **computer networks** have created **opportunities for crime** that never existed before, and, as a result, the police and justice departments are becoming increasingly concerned about the growing number of computer users who are **gaining access to** private or **secret information.** It's a problem that is on the rise worldwide. **Statistics** are showing a trend toward more computer crime every year.

As we all know, the information that passes through computer networks can be sensitive and even **dangerous** if the wrong people get access to it. *War Games*, a 1980's movie, illustrates this point very well. In *War Games*, a young high school boy gains access to the United States' **computerized military defense system** with the intention of playing a game, but ends up nearly starting a nuclear war. This theme is, of course, exaggerated . . . it is very unlikely that anyone, much less a high school boy, could penetrate the U.S. **military security** system, which limits access to sensitive networks within the government.

But the idea behind the movie is a disturbing one. People can and, in fact, are using their expertise in computer operations to break into computer networks . . . and are causing a lot of inconvenience and, even worse, are committing crimes and exposing others to danger. The point is this: . . . Computer crime is very real and dangerous.

Computer crime is tempting for two reasons: number one, some computer **geniuses** have trouble resisting the challenge—just to see if they can do it; and number two, computer crime sometimes has some very **significant rewards.**

Narrator: Stop the tape and answer the questions for Part 1. . . . Listen next to Part 2 of the lecture in which some different kinds of computer crimes and the problems they have caused are described.

PART 2

Now, so you don't get the wrong idea, let's refer to these people as **hackers**, because all of them are not criminals. Hackers basically fall into three categories: those who are **out for gain**, usually material or **financial**; those who are just plain **malicious** and are trying to hurt someone or cause someone more work; and those who simply do it for the fun or the challenge and don't want to hurt anyone, even though, in fact, they might. I think you can see the differences. The most dangerous by far are those who are out for material or financial gain . . . this kind of hacking also causes the biggest problems . . . but the most common hacker is the person who does it for the challenge or fun of it.

Let's look at the first type—the people who do this for financial gain. Banks, **insurance companies**, and **business organizations** utilize computers for most of their transactions. Most of their information is kept in computer files, making them the **hardest hit by** hackers.

This is how a typical hacking episode might go . . . a hacker figures out how to get into a bank network, changes account names and numbers, and diverts money into a bank account that has already been opened. The hacker then withdraws the money from the account, which is, of course, not in his or her real name. This hacking has just made that person rich. . . . In case you were wondering, this has actually happened many times in the past.

In companies, goods are stolen and **inventory** and **sales figures** are adjusted to **cover up** the problem. Mailing addresses are temporarily changed so that expensive or valuable items are sent to the hacker's address. The accounts are then changed back to the original addresses. Sometimes this type of robbery is not **detected** for months or years. Sometimes it is impossible to track down the criminal because the records have been changed back. These things are not just stories . . . these things have really happened.

Think about this for a moment . . . the American banking system alone **transfers** over 400 billion dollars *every day*. With this amount being transferred daily, it is no wonder that experts fear that a major **financial disaster** could occur. You may be interested to know that between 1 and 3 billion dollars are lost each year in the United States through computer crime, and 40 percent of large American companies suffered at least one major computer **fraud** in the last ten years. We can see from these figures how serious a problem this is.

And it's not only money that is stolen this way. The **theft** of information is also usually **financially motivated**. Some companies try to gain information about their competitors by accessing information from computers. Hackers also access and steal information in order to sell it to other people or competing companies. Again, their ultimate purpose is usually financial gain.

Not all hacking is malicious, of course, nor is it always financially motivated; much of it, in fact, most of it, is done purely for fun, or because the user enjoys the challenge of figuring out a computer's system. However, even when the purpose isn't malicious, the results of hacking can be very dangerous and tragic.

In June of 1983, for example, a hacker got into the computer at New York's **Memorial Sloan-Kettering Cancer Center**. This computer monitors important **medical equipment**, keeps **patients' records**, and is also used by about eighty hospitals to check what **treatment** those patients should receive. The hacker erased part of the computer's memory. Fortunately, none of the 6,000 patients' files or records were changed, so nobody was given the wrong treatment; but clearly the situation could have ended in **tragedy**. The FBI eventually caught that hacker.

Narrator: Stop the tape and answer the questions for Part 2. . . . The lecturer will now go on to talk about some of the solutions to the problem of computer hacking.

PART 3

Let's talk a little now about what is being done to stop computer crime. First, the **courts** are getting much tougher on hackers. They are punishing computer criminals more severely. They are trying to send a strong message to potential criminals: Computer crime is serious. If you're caught doing it, you'll be punished. This is seen as a way of **preventing** hacking.

Computer security is getting more sophisticated. . . . It's being improved by using less obvious and less easily remembered **passwords** that **allow access** to systems. These passwords should be given to the minimum number of people.

Access-control software is becoming more common. This software limits the user's access to information as well as the operations the user can perform. So, for example, access-control software might only let users read certain files or programs, but not let them input data, and may keep them out of other files entirely.

Then there are "dial back" systems that ask the user or caller for a password. The system then checks the password in a **directory** and calls the user back at his or her telephone number. This stops hackers who are calling from another number from gaining access to the system.

Scrambling devices are also being developed by computer engineers. These devices **scramble** messages so that hackers can't understand them. Data can be unscrambled and used only if the **scrambling key** is known by the user. Scrambling is a very effective way of protecting information.

Audit trail software is also now available. **Audit trails** monitor the use of a computer and alert owners to any attempt to enter their computer system. It is usually possible to identify any user who gained access to the system and when the access occurred, making it possible to trace the hacker.

Well, those are some of the major things that are happening at the present time in order to decrease computer crime. None of them is completely satisfactory, but together they are certainly helping. These changes, as well as the improvements that are certain to come, should influence people to stop hacking by making it less profitable and more risky. Well, let's stop here for today.

Narrator: Stop the tape and answer the questions for Part 3.

UNIT 4 Memory: Our Key to Learning

Narrator: This is the kind of lecture you would hear in an introduction to psychology course. This lecture is concerned with memory: what it is, how to measure it, and how to improve it.

PART 1

Good afternoon, everyone. Today, I have the pleasure of introducing you to the basics of one of the most fascinating topics in the field of **psychology** . . . memory. What is memory? Where is memory? How does memory work? The research in this field is fascinating and immense. We'll discuss these things briefly this afternoon.

I'll begin by saying a few things about the three types of memory that we all have, and then about how memory is measured, and, finally, I'll talk about some methods for improving your memory.

All right. First of all, let's look at types of memory. There are many ways to **classify** memory, but one of the most common is to classify it based on time . . . based on time and **duration** of use. So typically, memory is generally divided into three types: **sensory memory**, **short-term memory**, and **long-term memory**. That's sensory, short-term, and long-term.

So, let's look at sensory memory. Sensory memory holds information for only an instant, just to register an **impression** on one or more of the **senses**—sight, hearing, touch, smell, and taste. Here's an example of a phenomenon that I'm sure you all have experienced. . . . Imagine that you are holding up a **lighted match** or a **sparkler** on a dark night. . . . OK, start to move it in circles slowly, watching

it carefully the whole time . . . pretty soon you aren't just seeing the match or the sparkler . . . you can see a full circle of light! It's actually just one point of light being moved around, but your memory of the **sensation** of the light forms the rest of the circle. That is sensory memory. You can hold something in your sensory memory for just a fraction of a second . . . then it **fades** away. Just where is this information held during that part of a second? Well, for **visual information**, the **retina**, or the back part of your eye, is one place. The second place is the part of your brain that receives the information from your eyes. This is called the **visual cortex**. This part of your brain, the visual cortex, is very **sensitive to light patterns** and shapes, and holds some of your sensory memories.

Narrator: Stop the tape and answer the questions for Part 1. . . . Now, let's continue. The lecturer will discuss two additional types of memory.

PART 2

Now, if you want to keep the information for longer than a second, you have to put it into your short-term memory. It's kind of like tossing a ball from one hand to the other hand. Short-term memory, the second type of memory, is **temporary**; it allows us to hold on to things for as long as we think about them, for as long as we are paying attention to them.

It's something like a kind of **temporary storage** place. Look at the simple math problem in your text: 44 plus 8 plus 10 plus 18. . . . Next, cover the problem or just look away, and figure out the answer. Now, don't look back . . . Do you all have the answer? . . . Uh, let's see . . . 44 plus 8 is 52 . . . plus 10 is 62 . . . plus 18 is 80. The answer is 80. Now, to figure out this problem, you had to use your short-term memory.

As you do the problem, you have to continue paying attention to the numbers in your memory, until you get the final answer. If you stop concentrating on these numbers, stop saying them to yourself, or stop **visualizing** them—whatever it is that you do personally to keep something in mind—you will forget them and be unable to solve the problem. Do you see how that works?

Here's one more example that involves reading. Look at this sentence: "You need to use your short-term memory to understand this sentence!" It's written down in your textbook. Why, you may wonder, do we need short-term memory to understand such a simple sentence? We need it because short-term memory holds the first part of the sentence while our eyes move on to the last part. Without our short-term memory, we would forget the first part of the sentence before we got to the end. Reading even short or simple passages would be impossible without a short-term memory.

Now you see how important short-term memory is, but our short-term memory is just like an echo. If short-term memory were all we had, we would be very **limited**. It would be almost impossible to function in a normal manner. Well, fortunately, we all have a long-term memory, which brings me to the third type of memory that we'll talk about today.

When most of you think about memory, this is the type that you are probably thinking about—long-term memory. Long-term memory is involved with information that is **stored** for **considerable lengths of time**.

For example, do you remember what you ate for breakfast today? What about the name of your best friend when you were six years old? I would bet that you do. This information is in your long-term memory. Even though the time is different—this morning or many years ago—long-term memory behaves in the same way. Memory that is tested after about one minute behaves in a very similar way to memory tested after a day, a week, or even years. There are some scientists who would say that all of these memories are part of our long-term memory, regardless of the differences in time. Do these memories change . . . and if so, how? Well, they do seem to change. We tend to add information to these memories and change them constantly.

What is the reason behind these changes? Our memory is designed to keep or **preserve meaning** . . . to keep or preserve meaning, not to keep impressions or images, but to keep meaning. For example, try to remember a conversation you had yesterday with a friend. Now, if you are like most people, you simply can't remember the exact words that you or your friend said, but I think you can definitely remember the main ideas discussed. Your memories of the points that were most important to you will be the clearest. You can remember the meaning of the conversation. This is the **essential** feature of long-term memory. OK, are there any questions about that?

Narrator: Stop the tape and answer the questions for Part 2. . . . Now, let's continue with Part 3. In this section, we will look at ways of measuring memory.

PART 3

OK, let's move on to ways of measuring memory. Just as we distinguished three types of memory, there are

three main ways of measuring how much a person remembers. The first of these methods is called **recall**. You practice recall many times every day. Here's what I mean. . . . Take out a blank sheet of paper. . . . OK, now look at the **word list** in your text: tuba, drum, and so on. . . . Read it silently to yourself . . . OK? . . . Have you looked at all of the words? . . . OK, you should have finished by now. Now, close your book. Write down the words you saw, as many as you can, on your paper . . . go ahead. . . . OK, that's a simple recall test. . . . Now, most of you probably remembered most of the words, but not all of them. Our memories, of course, are not perfect!

The second method of measuring memory is **recognition**. OK, you need another piece of paper . . . or just turn that one over. . . . All right. Now, look at the word list again . . . . Close your book. . . . Now, I'm going to say some words . . . you only have to write *Yes* or *No*—*yes* if the word I say is on the list, **no** if the word I say is not on the list. . . . Ready? . . . Here I go . . . piano? . . . violin? . . . flute? . . . trumpet? . . . baseball? . . . soccer? . . . circle? . . . square? . . . daisy? . . . OK, did you do that? The answers are yes, no, yes, no, yes, no, yes, yes, yes. That, friends, is a **recognition test**.

Question: Which was easier—the recall or the recognition test? Obviously, recognition is a lot easier for most of us than recall. Asking yourself "Have I seen this before?" is much easier than remembering exactly all the things that you saw.

Now the third basic method . . . This method is relearning . . . relearning. . . . In a relearning test, you would try to **memorize** the list of words. Then, you would not look at the list for a period of time, maybe a week. If you're like most people, you will naturally be unable to remember all of the words after a few days or so. Well, anyway, after a week, you come back. I give you the list again, and you look at the list a second time and try to relearn it. As you should suspect, most people relearn information faster than they learned it the first time. By measuring the time necessary for a person to relearn information, we can calculate how much he or she had stored in long-term memory the first time.

Narrator: Stop the tape and answer the questions for Part 3. . . . Now, let's listen to the final section of the lecture. This section discusses ways of improving memory.

PART 4

OK. Let's change topics a bit and talk about some **techniques** for remembering information. One popular method that many people use to help them remember things is called **mnemonics**, m-n-e-m-o-n-i-c-s. . . . It's an unusual spelling—from the Greek word for **remember** . . . mnemonics. . . . In the mnemonic method, people use rhymes, clues, mental pictures, acronyms, et cetera, to help them **associate** the new information with fixed information . . . information that they already know. This fixed information helps them to **recognize** the new information and, as we have seen, recognition is easier than recall.

Let me give you an example. When I was in junior high school, in **geography** class, we had to memorize the names of the **Great Lakes** . . . you know, the five huge lakes in the **Midwest** of the United States. . . . Everybody could remember two or three or four, but most of us couldn't remember them easily, so the teacher, Mrs. . . .—what was her name? I can't remember—told us to use a **mnemonic**. She said, "Just remember the word HOMES." This word—h-o-m-e-s—has the first letter of each of the lakes. *H* stands for Huron, *O* for Ontario, *M* for Michigan, *E* for Erie, and *S* for Superior. I use that mnemonic to this day and I have never forgotten the names of the Great Lakes . . . even though I seem to have forgotten the name of the teacher who taught them to me!

There are many other kinds of mnemonics, but I think you see what I mean.

OK, let's look at the second memory technique—**personalizing**. Personalizing is based on the idea that we remember best the things that interest us the most. . . . For example, say you want to memorize the **diameter** of the Earth . . . which is 12,754 kilometers. How can you remember this number . . . 12,754? Well, I use a personal method. When I was a boy, my family moved to a new house—the address was 754 Spring Street. . . . So I say to myself, "When I was 12 years old, I moved to 754 Spring Street." . . . This works for me because I am using personal information that is important to me to aid in remembering a bit of information that may not be as important or personal.

The third technique, and probably the most important technique . . . is **organization**. Organization is the major key to remembering. Have you ever studied a foreign language and tried to memorize a vocabulary list of **unrelated words**? It's difficult to do. Very difficult. One way to make this easier is to **rearrange** the words so that they have some **logical** organization. For example, look at the two vocabulary lists in your textbook. Both lists consist of words in Japanese, with English translations. Which list do you think would be easier to memorize . . . the list on the left or the list on the right? . . . Most likely you picked the one on the right. These words are organized by topic whereas the words on the left are just **random**, with no particular

order, no particular organization. The point is this: Our memories are not random. We do not effectively store memories randomly, as lists with no meaning. We can remember better when we organize information, when it's meaningful.

So, let's stop there for today. I certainly hope you'll put today's material in your long-term memory . . . or you're going to have a hard time with the test.

Narrator: Stop the tape and answer the questions for Part 4.

UNIT 5   The Filmmaking Process

Narrator: You are about to hear a lecture on filmmaking. This lecture will be in three parts. The lecturer will give you an overview of the various steps involved in creating a motion picture.

PART 1

Good morning, ladies and gentlemen! Let's start this introduction to filmmaking with a simple question: How many of you have seen a movie this week? It doesn't matter if it was at the theater or just on your own TV. . . . Uh-huh, just as I thought; almost all of you have.

Of course, most of us love the movies—the magic, the escape that they provide . . . but most of us rarely stop to think about the process of making a movie. Just what does it take to get that movie from the idea stage to the final product? What are the decisions that must be made? What problems are encountered? Exactly how does a movie studio go about making a movie? These are precisely the topics that we will be exploring today.

There are six basic steps that are normally followed in the production of a full-length film. I'll outline them for you.

The first step is rather obvious . . . to make a film you must have an idea . . . a story . . . some topic for the project. The studio must find a **property**. That's a key word, folks—property, p-r-o-p-e-r-t-y. You all know the common meaning of this word, of course, but in filmmaking the word *property* has a very specific meaning. A property is the story on which the movie will be based. OK, it's the story on which the movie is based. You are probably wondering why we call it a property. . . . Well, it belongs to someone; it is that person's "property" and must be acquired by the studio, sometimes for quite a large sum of money.

There are basically two kinds of properties. The first is an **original story** that has never appeared anywhere before—never been in a book, or magazine, or another film. In other words, the story was **intended** from **the very beginning** to be made into a movie.

Star Wars is one good example of this type of property—you *do* remember that famous **science fiction film**, don't you? Another example is *Back to the Future*—oh, and also *Rocky*. All of these were based on a story written only for the purpose of making a movie.

Actually though, the majority of properties, for famous films at least, come from **novels**, plays, or **musicals** that are already published. Examples of this type of property include *The Sound of Music*, which was originally a play, *Tess*, a famous novel, and *The Godfather*, which was also first a novel.

OK, that's step number one—finding a property.

Well, now we have the property. The next step is to prepare a **script** from that property. This part of the process can take several months, or sometimes even a year or more. It's quite a lengthy and **time-consuming** process. During this time, the **scriptwriter**, **producer**, and **director** usually work very closely with each other.

Recently, there has been a trend to also have the **original writer**, the original property owner, take part in the production of the script. This means that if the property is taken from a book or play, the original author of the book or play is involved in writing the script. This is a good trend, I think . . . who could possibly know the story better or understand it more clearly than its original creator?

Another **option**, however, is for directors to write scripts themselves. This often occurs because scriptwriters are not only responsible for the **dialogue**, but they also must **specify** what kind of **camera shots** they want used. For instance, in all **scenes**, and especially long scenes that don't have any dialogue, the scriptwriter must describe what the camera should focus on, what should be in the center of the shot, what mood the image should present. Directors have much more experience with camera work and often prefer to write the script themselves for this reason.

So that's step number two—writing the script.

Narrator: Stop the tape and answer the questions for Part 1. . . . Listen now to Part 2 of the lecture in which steps three and four of the film-making process are discussed.

Part 2

OK, now the script is finished and approved, and we are ready for the next step . . . a very critical step indeed—the casting of the film.

The success or failure of a movie can depend on the ability of the actors and actresses to convince us that they really are the characters that they are portraying. The producer and the director must choose the cast very, very carefully. This step of choosing the actors and actresses is called **casting**. Got it? Casting is choosing the actors and actresses, the cast of the movie.

There are, in general, two types of casting. The first and the most common approach is to build the movie around a **famous star**. It is obvious that having a well-recognized name in the cast is a great asset to the film. Having someone, like **Tom Cruise**, **Meryl Streep**, or **Harrison Ford** will automatically attract large numbers of their fans to the movie. And of course, the financial success of the movie depends on how many people come to see it.

Now, there is also a second type of casting, and it has worked very well at times. Although it is true that top stars can **attract audiences**, they are also very, very expensive. With this in mind, some producers and directors cast their movies with unknown actors and actresses . . . concentrating on who fits the part the best, not who has the biggest name.

Actually, this approach, as I said, can work quite well because sometimes a big star can actually **take attention away from** the story itself. In other words, the stars distract the audience! The audience focuses on the star, not on the story. One example of this second type of casting is the movie *E.T.*, which is, in fact, one of the most popular movies of all time.

Unknown child actors and actresses were hired and the movie centered around the story itself. The producer and director probably thought that unknown actors would make the movie more believable. A big star might have actually hurt that movie.

Well, on to the next step. . . .

After the casting has been completed, the fourth step, **filming** the movie, can begin. Filming any kind of major motion picture usually takes about six to eight months. Now, you might not know this, but filming rarely takes place in the same order as the story. The reason for shooting in a different time order is that all the scenes with a big star can be done first, or all the scenes shot at the same location can be filmed at the same time. So what happens is this: The order scenes are filmed in and the order they appear in the movie are almost always completely different. It would be inconvenient and costs would increase dramatically if scenes were filmed in the order that we see them in the finished movie.

The filming itself is done in two types of places. The first is studio buildings called **soundstages**. They were given this name because both pictures and dialogues are recorded there. These soundstages can be made to appear like almost anything—from a fourteenth-century town to a small hotel room.

In addition to soundstages, most movies are partially filmed **on location**—in a real setting. On location means that the actors, actresses, film crew, and other necessary personnel must travel to a place like, maybe, a South American jungle or downtown Paris—or wherever—for filming certain scenes.

This makes the movie more interesting and realistic. **Indoor scenes** can easily be filmed on a soundstage, but scenes that require **extensive** use of outdoor **scenery** or use famous places as backgrounds must be done on location to be realistic.

As you can imagine, the costs of filming on location are **enormous**. People and equipment must be flown to the place, **living accommodations** must be found, and food has to be provided for a large number of people. There are lots of **practical problems** like these. The added realism of filming on location adds a lot of expense to a film.

Narrator: Stop the tape and answer the questions for Part 2. . . . Next, listen to Part 3 of the lecture. In this part of the lecture, the final two film production steps are discussed.

PART 3

Well, now, when all of the scenes are filmed and the director is finally **satisfied**, the next step, **editing** the film, begins. Editing, like filming, is an extremely long process and can easily take several months to complete. The **primary job** of editing is to select the best shots, the most effective takes . . . and put them into the best possible order. This is an extremely **complicated** process. Just deciding which of the shots is the best shot is an enormous task since every scene may have been filmed several times and in a variety of ways. In addition to selecting **the best take**—the best **version** of a scene—the editor must also decide when a particular scene has **made its point** and it is time to move on to the next one. In addition, the editor must be very careful about the **tempo** of the movie—the timing, the **pace**. Is the film moving too slowly or too quickly? By making these decisions about where to cut a scene, the film editor clearly has a strong **influence** over the **pace** and the feeling of the film. The difference between a good and a bad film can be in the quality of the editing.

When the editing is finally finished, it is time for the last step to take place. The final step is **composing** the music for the film. If you listen closely to the **sound track**

on almost any movie, you'll realize that the **impact** of most films is greatly **enhanced** by the music. This is fun to do; you should try it some time—watch a film you have already seen and just focus on the music. You'll be amazed at how much influence the music has on the film! Consider, for example, the music for *Star Wars* composed by John Williams. That music was so grandiose and stirring . . . just listening to the theme music put the audience in a state of anticipation. It added a lot of excitement and emotion to the film.

Now, although composers would probably like to be hired in the early stages of a film—so that they can have more time to consider the mood of the story—in most cases the composer is hired only after most of the filming has been completed. The composer will write some music for the movie, which must be approved by the producer and director. The three of them will then consult on where in the film to include music.

Now, how do you think that the music is actually recorded? This is really interesting . . . the conductor must actually watch the film at the same time that he is conducting the orchestra! Of course, this is a difficult, time-consuming process that requires careful planning beforehand. Perhaps you've seen this before on TV or somewhere.

OK, so those are the basic steps. Let's review them quickly.

First, find the property. Then, second, a script must be written . . . by the director, or often by the original author, who knows the story best. Third, the movie is then cast—remember, that means finding actors and actresses to play the roles. The next step, filming, follows. For most films, this takes around six months and is done on location or in soundstages, or both. After that, the editing can be done—selecting the best takes. And finally, the last step is composing music for the movie.

As I briefly mentioned, costs can soar in filmmaking, especially if a lot of special effects and big name stars are used. As a small item of information to finish with: What do you think was the most expensive film ever made? Well, you probably didn't guess this one. The most expensive film ever made was *Cleopatra*, which was filmed in 1963. The cost—in 1992 dollars—was $194 million. Another expensive movie was *Terminator 2*, which was filmed in 1990—with Arnold Schwarzenegger. This was said to have cost over $100 million. That, ladies and gentlemen, is a lot of money.

Narrator: Stop the tape and answer the questions for Part 3.

UNIT 6 Non-Verbal Communication: Your Body is Talking

Narrator: This is the kind of lecture you would hear in an introductory psychology course. This lecture is concerned with non-verbal communication and how it differs from verbal communication.

PART 1

OK, everyone, let's talk about communication. When I say "communication," most of you probably think about **verbal communication**—that is, the words we use when we talk to someone. However, there is another important **aspect** to communication: **non-verbal communication,** which is communication done by using our bodies, **gestures,** and tones of voice—simply everything except the actual words we use. As you will see, in many ways this non-verbal communication is more important than our verbal communication.

What is non-verbal communication and how do we study it? Actually, non-verbal communication is a rather recent field of study. Originally, scientists called this field **kinesics.** That's spelled k-i-n-e-s-i-c-s. This may be a new word for you. Kinesics is the scientific study of **body movements** used in communication. By movements, I mean gestures, **facial expressions,** eye behavior—the **gaze** of the eyes—and **posture.** In addition to these movements, we also communicate with our **speech rate**—that is, how fast we talk—and the volume of our speech—how loudly we talk. Non-verbal communication **encompasses** a wide range of actions.

Um, the field of kinesics owes a great deal to one man: **Raymond Birdwhistle**—that's right, his name is Bird-whistle—B-i-r-d-w-h-i-s-t-l-e—that should be easy for you to remember! Birdwhistle was quite a famous American **anthropologist.** He **estimated** that about 70 percent of what is communicated in a conversation is non-verbal. Birdwhistle began his studies of non-verbal communication in the early 1950s and since he established this field of study as a legitimate one, many other anthropologists and **psychologists** have devoted their time to non-verbal communication.

In any case, let's look more closely at some of Birdwhistle's ideas. . . . It was Birdwhistle's belief that the **meaning** of non-verbal **behavior** depended on the **context** in which it occurred . . . the meaning of non-verbal behavior depends on context.

Because of this belief, he was very concerned with looking at the whole context of non-verbal behavior—how and where certain types of non-verbal behavior appeared, not just the particular behavior alone. Take facial expressions, for example— **frowns, smiles, raised eyebrows,** and so on—we all use these things to convey many different meanings. However, those meanings are **determined** largely by the situations that we are in and by the **relationships** we have with the people we are communicating with. In other words, the same expressions, say a smile or a frown, can have different meanings.

What does a smile mean? What does it mean if I smile at you? Well, it could mean that I like you. That would be a kind of **affection.** It could mean I'm just trying to make you feel **comfortable.** That might be a way of being **polite.** It might mean I think you said something silly or funny. That would be a kind of **feedback.** The point is that the **situation** or the relationship of the people involved determines the meaning of the smile.

Narrator: Stop the tape and answer the questions for Part 1. . . . Let's continue with Part 2 in which we will hear about three differences between verbal and non-verbal communication.

PART 2

Next, let's take a few minutes to explain how verbal and non-verbal communication differ. Actually, I would like to go into five different points.

The first point I would like to discuss is that, uh, whereas spoken languages differ between countries, or even from one place to another within the same country, many people believe that most non-verbal communication is kind of natural, um, and not learned and is, therefore, **universal** and not totally dependent on our place of birth or the verbal language that we speak. Most people seem to think that all non-verbal communication is the same everywhere. . . . That is not true . . . it is not identical the world over, but some striking similarities do exist.

Basic **emotions** *are*, however, communicated in essentially the same non-verbal way throughout the world. Accordingly, these emotions are called **universal emotions**. Examples include emotions such as happiness, sadness, fear, anger—things like that. Humans all over the world—humans from different **cultures**—express these emotions in the same non-verbal ways, although they may have different words for the emotion. Fear, for example, is universally expressed by opening the eyes very wide, opening the mouth, and so on.

Although we do have these universal emotions, it's also important to note that many non-verbal expressions of ideas and protocol do often **vary** from one culture to the next, as I'm sure you've noticed if you have traveled at all. Think about how people from different cultures act when they meet for the first time. This type of greeting is done very differently depending on where they are. In some cultures people **shake hands**, while in others people **bow**. Some people may **hug**, and yet others may make a particular hand gesture when they first meet.

Second, although we know a great deal about the system that spoken language uses, namely **grammar**, we still do not know a lot about non-verbal rules in any one society, much less how the rules might **interact** across cultures. In other words, scientists have yet to fully understand the "grammar" of non-verbal communication. A big problem in figuring out this non-verbal grammar is that it is **ambiguous**: As Birdwhistle said back in the 50s, the same non-verbal action can mean many different things depending on the situation or the culture. This is not as much of a problem in spoken language because it is less ambiguous. Non-verbal communication may never be fully understood.

The third difference is that we have **dictionaries** for spoken language where we can look up any unknown word and have the meaning explained to us. There is nothing like that for non-verbal communication. The vocabulary of spoken language is somehow clearer, or at least easier to write down, than that of non-verbal communication. Let's look at an example. If you go to a foreign country and somebody makes a hand gesture that you don't understand, can you check a book for the meaning of that gesture? Generally speaking, it is impossible. Dictionaries or reference books for these non-verbal meanings just don't exist, at least not yet.

However, that gesture has meaning just as a word has meaning. Sometimes, the same gesture even has different meanings in different cultures. Here in the United States we make a circle with our thumb and first finger and this means "OK." In Japan this means "money," and in South America this gesture has a **sexual meaning**. There's a funny, or actually **embarrassing** story about this particular gesture—former President **Richard Nixon** made **a huge mistake** when, on a trip to South America, he held up both hands using this OK gesture. Of course, the people in the audience were shocked because it meant something entirely different than OK to them! This example shows us that we have to be awfully careful about what our bodies are saying . . . especially when we travel outside our own culture.

Narrator: Stop the tape and answer the questions for Part 2. . . . Let's continue with Part 3 in which we'll hear about the last two differences between verbal and non-verbal communication.

PART 3

Now, let's go on to the fourth difference. **Clarification** . . . although we can ask for clarification or **repetition** of what someone says, it is practically impossible to do the same with non-verbal communication. For example, it would be very strange to ask, "Could you repeat that smile again?" or "What does that facial expression mean?" Thus, we have to understand non-verbals the first time. Repetition is generally not a possibility. This is clearly very different from spoken language where we often ask for repetition.

To finish up, although we can **conceal** our true thoughts and feelings with spoken language, it's difficult or maybe even impossible to do so with non-verbal communication. For instance, we can't stop ourselves from **blushing** if we're embarrassed, or **sweating** if we're very **nervous**, and we can't slow down our **heartbeat** if we're scared. Because of this, sometimes the things we say and the things our bodies say . . . our verbal and non-verbal communication . . . are different.

Let's take an easy example. You see your friend who is sweating and looking very worried so you ask, "What's wrong?" Your friend answers, "Nothing." Do you believe him? Of course not! When this happens, we will always believe the non-verbal communication. Non-verbals are more honest, you see.

OK. Uh, so to briefly **recap** what I've said here, we looked at five differences between verbal and non-verbal communication. The first was, uh, the idea that non-verbal communication is more natural, more universal than verbal communication. Secondly, we don't know much about the system or "grammar" of non-verbal communication. The third point was, uh, let me see, oh, yes, we don't have dictionaries to explain the meaning of non-verbals like we do for spoken language. Next, uh, number four has to do with the idea of repetition. It's more difficult or maybe impossible to ask someone to repeat or clarify a gesture or facial expression. And lastly, we need to remember that non-verbal communication is more honest than verbal communication. We, well, most people, anyway, can't hide their emotions very successfully non-verbally. Our eyes or our faces will give away our real feelings. All right. I think that pretty well covers it. Are there any questions now?

Narrator: Stop the tape and answer the questions for Part 3.

UNIT 7 Effects of the Sun

Narrator: This is the type of lecture you would hear in a public health course. This lecture is about the dangers of exposure to the sun and ways to protect our health from those dangers.

PART 1

Hello, everyone. In our last class we talked about some of the important benefits of sunlight and, in particular, about the role the sun plays in the production of vitamins, such as vitamin D.

Today's discussion will focus instead on the adverse effects that the sun can have on our health. As **exposure** to the sun and associated problems are increasing, it is vital that anyone interested in public health or health education be up-to-date on this issue. Today's talk, again, is going to be about some of the dangers of exposure to the sun.

For many years now, a lot of people have tried to darken their skin color, have tried to tan their bodies. It's considered to be beautiful and a sign of fitness, good health, youth, and sometimes even economic or financial success . . . for many white people, a tan in the winter means that they can afford to vacation someplace exotic. Unfortunately, however, a lot of people don't realize that exposure to very **direct sunlight** or exposure for great lengths of time can be extremely dangerous—too much sunlight is a **potential cause** of **cancer**.

As future health educators, I think you should all be aware of these dangers, and so today I want to go into some detail about this growing problem. First, I'll talk a bit about the extent of this problem, then, who is in the greatest danger, and finally, how we can protect ourselves from the sun.

It's been quite recently, just since the 1980s, that we started hearing just how bad the sun can be for the skin—and it's surprising to me to see millions of people still on beaches every summer, or working out in the sun for hours and hours. I guess many of these people don't know what a **risk** they are taking. According to some of the experts, the people who do these things are playing a game of "solar roulette." Roulette, for those of you who don't know, is a popular gambling game, and people who sunbathe are gambling with their lives.

Listen to this . . . this year alone, more than 600,000 cases of **skin cancer** will be reported, most of them caused by too much exposure to **ultraviolet rays** from the sun. Can you believe that?! Around 30,000 of these cases will be the most dangerous kind of cancer, called **melanoma**, and approximately 6,500 people will die from it. These kinds of statistics should really make us appreciate the dangers of the sun. In the United States we know that about one out of every six people will develop some form of skin cancer and that more than 90 percent of those cases will be directly related to exposure to the sun. That should give you some idea of the large scope of the problem we're dealing with.

Narrator: Stop the tape and answer the questions for Part 1. . . . Let's continue with the lecture. In this section, the lecturer explains who is most likely to have difficulty with exposure to the sun.

PART 2

All right. Let's talk a little about who is most likely to suffer from the most serious form of skin cancer—melanoma. There are three major factors that raise a person's risk of getting melanoma at some point in his or her life.

First, there is a **hereditary** factor. Hereditary factors are factors you are born with—your general **genetic** makeup, things like your skin and hair color. In general, **light-skinned**, **light-eyed people** of **northern European background** are most likely to suffer from skin cancer. These people often have red or blond hair, and freckled skin that turns red and burns easily. In contrast, dark-haired **Caucasians**, **Asians**, and **Hispanics** suffer less from this disease, and dark-skinned people are 50 times less likely than light-skinned people to contract melanoma. So the main idea is that light-skinned people and especially those with blond or red hair are **at risk**.

Second, there is the **environmental** factor. Where you live seems to influence your chances of contracting the disease . . . **geography** is associated with the incidence of skin cancer. The farther north or south of the **equator** you are, the less likely you are to get skin cancer because the **sun's rays** are not directly overhead, but instead hit the Earth at a softer **angle**. For example, someone who lives in southern Florida, which is fairly near the equator, is more likely to contract this disease than someone who lives in Alaska, where the sun's rays are never directly overhead. This means that the rays take longer to reach the Earth, so the **ozone** layer of the Earth's **atmosphere** is able to stop more of the sun's dangerous ultraviolet light. One interesting study I read recently, a comparison, showed that Japanese who live in Hawaii are 88 times more likely to get skin cancer than Japanese living in Japan. That in itself shows pretty clearly what a difference in geography and, probably, also a difference in **life-style** can make—I'm sure that living in Hawaii makes it more tempting to spend time at the beach.

So far we have one hereditary and one environmental factor.

The third factor is a **behavioral** factor . . . the history of the person . . . the amount of exposure to the sun that the person has had from birth on. In general, we can say, by referring to the research that has been done up to now, that it's quite clear that getting sunburned frequently and severely early in our lives can have **negative consequences** later on. This means that we need to ensure that parents, especially, are educated about the dangers of this problem so that they can try to keep their children protected. It also means that certain kinds of jobs—**outdoor jobs**—will put a person at greater risk.

Narrator: Stop the tape and answer the questions for Part 2. . . . Let's continue with Part 3. In this section, the lecturer will tell how to protect yourself from the sun.

PART 3

Well, we've described the problem and some of factors that contribute to the problem, but just what is it that we can do to improve this situation? As health workers, this is one of our responsibilities—what can we do to educate the public about this problem?

For one thing, we can make people more aware of the dangers of too much sunbathing. This is best done through the media—radio, TV, and newspapers, posters, pamphlets, and so on. You know the **American Cancer Society's** campaign—**"Fry Now, Pay Later"**—was very effective. It was kind of a **scare tactic**—trying to frighten people into action—but it was very effective.

Probably the most important breakthrough in sun protection and the best advice that we can offer to the public is this: Wear **sunscreen**. It's simple—wear sunscreen. Use a sunscreen with an **SPF rating** of at least 15. SPF means "sun protection factor." What does that 15 mean? Let's say on a hot day it would take your skin twenty minutes to begin to burn. A sunscreen with an SPF of 15 will allow you to stay in the sun fifteen times longer. Let's see, fifteen times twenty minutes would be, uh, three hundred minutes or, um, five hours, right? Yes, you could stay in the sun for around five hours and receive the same dose of **radiation**. That's a huge difference.

Also, when you buy sunscreen, it is essential that you purchase one that **filters out UVA** as well as **UVB light**. I should stop and explain that. UVA and UVB light are the types of ultraviolet rays that can burn you. A good sunscreen has filters for UVA and UVB light.

The next piece of advice is to put on the sunscreen at least fifteen to thirty minutes before going out into the sun. Why so long beforehand? The reason is that it takes most sunscreens about fifteen minutes to react with your skin and form a **protective coating**. Also, you should reapply the sunscreen after exercising and especially after swimming. Even if you're just lying in the sun, you should reapply your sunscreen once every two hours.

Finally, you have to pay attention to sensitive areas that are easy to miss when you put on sunscreen. For example, be careful to get enough on your ears, neck, lips, nose, and, yes, you men out there, any bald spots on your head. These places on your face and head tend to be missed and, as they are hit by the sun very directly, can burn quickly.

So, to summarize, a well-protected person will do several things: (1) use a sunscreen with a rating of at least 15; (2) get a sunscreen that contains UVA and UVB protections; (3) put on plenty of sunscreen about thirty minutes before going into the sun; and (4) pay attention to sensitive areas. That's pretty simple advice, but it can make a lot of difference. It may even save your life.

Well, I'll stop here for now and see if you have any questions.

Narrator: Stop the tape and answer the questions for Part 3.

UNIT 8 Mystics and Prophets

Narrator: This is the type of lecture you would hear in a philosophy class or a class on world religions. The lecture concerns mysticism and one mystic in particular, Nostradamus.

PART 1

Good morning, everyone. After our lecture last week on **prophets** and **prediction**, many of you came up to me and asked me if I would, uh, give a short talk on the famous prophet, **Nostradamus**. So I've decided to spend a little time doing that today.

First, I'd like to review what I said last time about prophets and, particularly, **mystics**. If you remember, I told you that we can classify prophets as one of two types. The first type is what we might call a **divine prophet**, or religious prophet, if you like. A divine prophet or a religious prophet is an inspired teacher or, uh, a messenger who communicates to us and **interprets** God's will, God's messages to us. These prophets are the ones who establish the great religions of the world.

The major prophets of this kind have been Zoroaster, Buddha, Moses, Jesus Christ, Muhammed, and Bahaullah. These prophets came to Earth in order to deliver divine or religious messages . . . to communicate to us humans how to live on Earth. Divine prophets bring laws and so on. A society is usually formed around the teachings that they bring.

The other kind of prophet, the second kind of prophet, is really better termed a mystic. A mystic is a person who has **visions** and makes predictions about the future . . . and claims to know what will happen.

Mystics seem to share two things—that is, they have two things in common. First, they do not generally seem to be directly concerned with the problems of this world. . . . It is somehow as if they are **detached** . . . or not connected to the day-to-day problems of living . . . and they personally don't seem to have the **selfish needs** and desires of most people. In a word, they're different. Being detached makes them different.

Second, mystics seem to experience a kind of **spiritual union** with some **higher power**. They claim to be in some kind of contact with a power or force that is greater than most humans experience, and they all seem to have **direct knowledge** of a **spiritual reality** that exists outside of our everyday world. By *spiritual reality* we mean "God," or the supreme creative force in the universe, whatever we may call it. This connection is where they claim that their knowledge comes from.

Now, what *direct knowledge* seems to mean is not that mystics hear strange or mysterious voices or see unusual signs. Rather, it seems to mean knowledge they have obtained without using the senses—a direct spiritual link up, you might say.

Now sometimes, because mystics are in contact with a spiritual reality, they may not have words to use to describe what they are experiencing, and so what they say often sounds like nonsense to us . . . the vocabulary that they need hasn't been invented yet! For instance, Nostradamus made some predictions over 400 years ago, and he actually made up words to describe the things he was seeing. For example, he had a vision of a submarine, but, of course, submarines didn't exist then, so he said things like, and I quote, "iron fish enclosing men, usually traveling with a **warlike intent**." And for most people, this didn't make any sense at all. So the point here is that in order to understand mystics, we often have to use our **imagination**.

Narrator: Stop the tape and answer the questions for Part 1. . . . Now, let's continue with Part 2. In this section, we will hear briefly about Nostradamus's life.

PART 2

Let me turn the discussion to the topic of Nostradamus himself, and say a couple of things about his life and his work. . . . Nostradamus lived from 1503 to 1566 and was a doctor and **astrologer**—an astrologer, of course, is a person who studies the stars—or heavens, if you like—and makes predictions based on the position of the stars.

Anyway, Nostradamus studied **medicine** at **Montpellier** . . . don't worry about the spelling of that right now . . . Montpellier was the second-best French university, **Paris** being the best. Nostradamus spent much of his life moving around France from place to place and became known for his efforts to help sufferers of **the plague**, a deadly **disease** that killed millions of people in Europe in the **Middle Ages**. To many people, Nostradamus was a hero, and from what we know of him, he certainly was a kind and helpful person. In this sense, maybe, he was a bit different from many mystics—he wasn't quite so detached.

Anyway, it seems that his prophetic powers—his ability to make prophecies—began to appear around 1550, around the time he was fifty years old. Little by little, his **fame** as an astrologer and as a mystic began to grow . . . first in France and then abroad . . . and he began to spend a lot of his time making **horoscopes** for visitors. Horoscopes, as you probably know, are meant to give people some insight into their own characters or personalities and often make predictions about the future.

But to continue here, many of Nostradamus's visitors were **royalty**—kings and queens, and princes and princesses . . . such as the then queen of France, **Catherine de Medici**. These famous visitors went to Nostradamus to ask for mystic visions of the future. So clearly, Nostradamus was quite well-known in his own time as well.

In addition to making horoscopes for the rich and famous, Nostradamus was also busy writing down his prophecies in his two most famous books, *Prophecies* and *Centuries*. Did you get those? . . . *Prophecies* and *Centuries*.

Narrator: Stop the tape and answer the questions for Part 2. . . . Let's continue with Part 3, in which we will hear about two of Nostradamus's prophecies.

PART 3

So, what were some of the prophecies of Nostradamus? Why are people still interested in him even today, over 400 years after his death? Nostradamus made many predictions in his books that seem to have been proven correct—for example, those relating to the British queen, Elizabeth I, to the French scientist, Louis Pasteur, and to other famous people. However, the most compelling reason that Nostradamus is still receiving a lot of attention is because of his so-called **negative predictions**—his predictions of future tragedies and disasters. Tragedies and disasters seem to catch people's interest!

One disaster that people claim that Nostradamus foresaw was the dropping of the two atomic bombs on **Hiroshima** and **Nagasaki** at the end of World War II. Nostradamus predicted that, quote, "near the **harbor** and in two cities, two scourges will fall, unlike anything seen before." **Scourge** means something that causes great pain and suffering. Both cities, in case you didn't know, are next to the ocean. Hiroshima borders the Japanese **Inland Sea** and Nagasaki is on the **Pacific Ocean**, so the reference to the harbor makes sense. He said there would be hunger and disease as a result of these scourges, and that people would cry to God for help. That description is a fitting one for the disasters at Hiroshima and Nagasaki.

Nostradamus also spoke of an emperor, quote ,"born near Italy who will cost the **empire** very dearly." **Napoleon** was born in **Corsica** near Italy, and his politics and fighting certainly did cost the French empire dearly; in fact, his actions almost completely destroyed it in the end. In his writings, Nostradamus talks about "PAU NAY LORON." That's P-A-U . . . N-A-Y . . . L-O-R-O-N. Now, if the order of these letters is changed around, they spell *Napaulon Roy*, or "Napoleon the King" in English. In Nostradamus's time, Napoleon's name was often spelled with "au" rather than "o," and so this is often thought to show that Nostradamus knew about the coming of Napoleon.

OK. We have discussed three specific prophecies of Nostradamus's—for each one, the actual prediction is somewhat **vague**, but for each one, there is a good deal of **evidence** to suggest that Nostradamus was a mystic with a real vision of the future.

Let me say one more thing before I finish. Many of the writings of Nostradamus are even less clear, even more difficult to interpret than the examples I've given you here . . . so I'd like to finish by saying once again that we must be very careful about any conclusions we arrive at regarding the writings of Nostradamus. You know, some people

claim that Nostradamus's followers are just bending history to fit his predictions. . . . Which is true? Is he a prophet or a fraud? . . . You will have to make up your own mind about that one!

OK, that's about all the time I want to take today on the topic of mystics and predictions. Be sure to finish Chapter 17 by the next class.

Narrator: Stop the tape and answer the questions for Part 3.

UNIT 9 The Biological Clock

Narrator: The lecture you are about to hear is from a health sciences course. It concerns the problem of aging and reviews some of the basic research that is being done. The research is focused on trying to find out why we age and how the aging process might be slowed down.

PART 1

Good afternoon, everyone. Today's lecture will be devoted to a topic that I think will be of interest to all of you. This topic is: aging, spelled a-g-i-n-g, kind of an unusual word. Anyway, we will take a look at some of the reasons why the body ages and we will also discuss a promising discovery that may contribute to slowing down the **aging process**.

Small groups of scientists in Russia and in the United States have been researching this field for the past few years. These scientists have uncovered some fascinating truths about aging. The discoveries that have been made will, of course, be important in the treatment of age-related illness, but more importantly this could have a powerful impact on medicine and society as a whole. Now that I hope I have you interested, let's get on to the details!

The first and most basic question is: Why do we age? Does anyone really know the answer? Well, up to recently, the most popular theories held that it's because our bodies simply **wear out**, like engines or any other types of machines that are used for a long time. Of course, if we think about this for a moment, we realize that this can't be the whole reason. . . . Athletes, for instance, run and work out, train, and use their bodies much more than most of us, and their bodies don't seem to wear out faster—in fact, their bodies seem to last longer than those of people who don't exercise. . . . So, mechanical reasons can't be the only reason that we age.

In addition to simple **mechanical wear and tear**, there must be another, more important reason. Research has led us to believe that each of the body's **cells** contains a kind of clock . . . the entire body has a kind of built-in clock—a **biological clock**, if you will. This biological clock is always ticking—tick-tick-tick—and it controls the processes and changes in each individual cell. The clock ticks on, a person ages, and, of course, eventually dies.

Now, imagine you could find a way to slow down this clock—so that instead of tick-tick-tick, the clock was going tick-tick-tick—then your biological . . . your aging time would slow down in comparison to real time . . . and you would age more slowly. Slowing down the rate of your biological clock is the true key to longer life.

The first thing you need to understand is that the speed of our biological clocks is **influenced by hormones**, and particularly the hormones from the **pituitary gland**—pituitary . . . gland, that's p-i-t-u-i-t-a-r-y—a small, oval-shaped gland at the base of the brain. This gland is very little . . . and hugely important . . . and for some reason, after we turn, well, from around the time that we turn twenty, our pituitary glands begin to **secrete** a hormone called **DECO**—D-E-C-O— into our blood. This stands for "**Decreasing Consumption of Oxygen.**" *Decreasing* . . . that's the *DE, Consumption,* that's the *C* . . . and *Oxygen* . . . that's the *O*. D-E-C-O. Now, interestingly, this hormone is often called the "**death hormone.**" Why do you think it's called the death hormone? Well, let's think about that—if you can't get any **oxygen**, if, for example, someone starts to choke you . . . you can't breathe . . . what happens next? No oxygen to your blood, no oxygen to the cells of your **brain** and your other organs, and you are dead.

Well, with DECO, it's not that sudden; the effect is much slower. It takes many years for DECO to weaken our bodies little by little by supplying them with less oxygen . . . and having less oxygen **impairs** or weakens a number of our **bodily functions**. Even worse, the amount of DECO that we secrete increases as we age. If you think about that, we are all killing ourselves. A somewhat surprising and shocking situation, isn't it?

So, to sum up this idea, most of the effects of aging can be traced to the secretion of DECO. In some Russian and American **laboratory experiments**, the scientists devised an experiment using laboratory animals—some white rats had the DECO hormone removed . . . **eliminated**. . . . What do you think happened to these rats? Yes, that's right

. . . they actually seemed to grow younger . . . not grow older . . . they grew younger! The **hearts** and **lungs** of these rats became as strong as those of younger rats. In addition, their **immune systems** became much more capable of **fighting infection**.

So, what does this mean to us humans? Well, if we can discover an **antidote** to DECO, something that will destroy DECO or prevent our bodies from producing it, we should be able to live longer. Right now, from my understanding of the research, it looks like an antidote to DECO may be ready within the next ten years or so. What a miracle drug that would be if it really worked. But, there is an aging problem other than DECO.

Narrator: Stop the tape and answer the questions for Part 1. . . . Listen now to Part 2. In this part, you will hear about a second major factor in the aging process.

PART 2

This other problem is the second point that I would like to cover today. Unfortunately, scientists have, as yet, no power to fight this cause of aging. The problem relates to the normal process of cellular replacement. As I am sure you remember from last week's lecture, all of the cells in our bodies are regularly dying and being replaced. The important question is, however, how long can cells keep on reproducing? For how many **generations** will cells reproduce before they simply die out?

So, many researchers are asking, is there is a limit to our **supply of cells**? Is there a limit to the number of **generations** a cell can have? If there is, can we extend the number of generations that our cells will reproduce? In the late 1950s and early 1960s, a **Dr. Leonard Hayflick** of **Stanford University** was one of the early pioneers in this area of aging. He found out that there was, unfortunately, a limit. That limit for most cells is approximately fifty generations.

For example, he found that the hair cells of most men will keep on reproducing for maybe forty or fifty generations, and then they simply stop—the man begins to go bald. This is, of course, an inconvenience, not a life-threatening problem, but when the cells of our skin or vital organs stop reproducing, that is life-threatening. Our vital organs will therefore inevitably wear out and we will die.

In his experiments, Dr. Hayflick discovered the reason: There seems to be a "program," or set of instructions in the **genetic code** of the cell, located somewhere in the cell's **nucleus**. This program, or the genetic code, sets a limit to the number of times a cell can divide. Right now, it appears that even if the problem of DECO is solved, this program located in our cells will be the final **barrier** that will prevent humans from living extremely long lives.

Narrator: Stop the tape and answer the questions for Part 2. . . . Let's continue with Part 3, which will be a very short section. In this section, the lecturer will discuss the moral and ethical problems of slowing down aging.

PART 3

Well, we've seen two of the reasons that we age—our secretion of DECO and the genetic code in our cells that limits the number of times that the cells can reproduce. Can we **overcome** these problems? Can we get beyond these barriers?

Well, I think the answer is "yes." . . . An antidote to DECO is already being experimented with. Perhaps people who take this antidote will live longer lives. . . . And we are seeing some early experiments in changing the genetic code in cells, changing the instructions that nature has given to the cells. So, the answer must be "yes"—in our lifetimes we will see ways of slowing down the aging process. But, of course, the scientific part of the question is only one side of the question. Once the scientific problems are solved, our society will have to face the **moral** and ethical problems that will be raised by this technology. For example, should we be tampering with nature's plan for humans? Should we be trying to live longer than nature intended? Who receives the treatments . . . and for what price? And on the social side, is it necessarily a good thing for people to live 100, 125, or 150 years? Can the planet support the increase in population . . . and pollution?

These are difficult **philosophical** and moral questions . . . and sometimes the philosophical questions are more difficult than the scientific ones. We do know this: There won't be any easy answers, but it is important for all of us to begin thinking about these issues now.

Well, I hope that gives you something to think about this week. I think we can stop here for today.

Narrator: Stop the tape and answer the questions for Part 3.

UNIT 10 The First Year of Life

Narrator: This is the kind of lecture you might hear in a child development class. This lecture concerns the first six months of infant development.

PART 1

OK, is everyone ready? As I told you last time, today's lecture is about babies. We'll start from birth—what **newborn** babies know and are capable of immediately after they are born—and then talk about how they **develop** during the first six months of their lives.

Until recently, it was difficult for researchers to know what babies were feeling or experiencing because, well, the researchers just didn't have any way to communicate with the babies. After all, it wasn't like the babies could just answer questions about what they knew or how they felt! Researchers pretty much had to guess what babies were experiencing. However, technology has made rapid progress in the last several years and scientists have utilized this new technology to understand far more about how babies develop.

A baby's development is divided into two basic **skill areas** for the purpose of observation and testing. These two areas are **motor skills**, which involve **physical development** such as **rolling over**, sitting up, **picking up objects**, and drawing, and second, **language-interaction skills**, which involve comprehending others' language and interacting with others—how the baby socializes. OK, so today we will track a baby's development in these skill areas—motor development and language interaction. In addition to these two skill areas, we will also track the development of babies' vision.

Generally, for all babies, there are basic **patterns of development** for motor skills. They develop from **gross movements**—very large movements—to **delicate movements**—very small movements—and from trunk to outer limbs and from head to toe. So, for example, a gross movement would be rapidly moving the arm up and down; a delicate movement would be using the thumb and first finger to pinch something. Do you see the distinction there? From gross to delicate movements, and from trunk to outer limbs! Babies learn to control their heads before they walk . . . like I said, from head to toe.

In terms of language interaction, the general movement, the general pattern of development is from **responding** to language to **initiating an interaction** . . . from responding to initiating.

Now, these are just general patterns of development. . . . Let's look at some specific developments in babies.

Narrator: Stop the tape and answer the questions for Part 1. . . . Now, let's listen to Part 2 in which we will hear about the next stage of development.

PART 2

But before going any further, I'd like to mention something about—quote—"normal development." I'd like to emphasize that "normal development" in any individual baby can be quite different from the average ages I'm going to give you. For example, while most babies will learn to sit up at around six months of age, it wouldn't be unusual if a baby learned to do so at five months or even eight months. There is a big variation in these normal ages.

All right, so, uh, let's begin with, uh, newborns. In terms of motor control, newborns can move their arms and legs with gross movements, and, in addition, move them away from anything that is uncomfortable, such as something too hot or cold. OK? That's pretty basic. They can also lift their heads and **turn their heads from side to side**—they are developing from head to toe, right? As for their **eye movements**, **focusing on** things eight to twelve inches away from their faces is no problem, and they can occasionally get their hands into their mouths.

In terms of language interaction, they respond to sounds and, in particular, they respond to their own mothers' voices. This is probably due to the fact that babies, even while they are still in their mothers' wombs, can hear their mothers' voices well enough to distinguish them from other people's voices.

When we think about **social awareness**, which is the beginning of interaction, it's interesting to note that newborns have been shown to prefer looking at real live human faces rather than **inanimate** objects, such as pictures. And they very much respond to **human touch** by **cuddling** against whomever is holding them. OK, so the main observation here is that newborns are very actively developing their skills, both their motor skills and their social language skills.

Because babies develop so rapidly, we can see some distinct changes by two months of age. Their motor control has improved . . . to the point that they can push their heads and chests up while lying on their stomachs. This is a big, a major development that has the effect of making babies feel very powerful! In addition, their neck muscles are getting stronger every day, so their heads become much steadier and don't bob around so much.

Narrator: Stop the tape and answer the questions for Part 2. . . . Let's continue with Part 3 in which we will hear about infants' development at two and four months of age.

PART 3

At this age babies can **follow an object** with their eyes from left to right or from right to left a full **90 degrees**. In addition, they can distinguish between shapes and colors with their eyes. You may also notice that infants at this age are starting to be able to bring their hands together. This is important because soon they will gain the skill of **grasping** objects . . . picking up their favorite toys . . . or anything else that gets their attention.

Their language and social interaction are also developing . . . they are beginning to **coo** and make **vowel sounds** like "ooh," "aah," and "eeh." They respond when you talk to them by cooing, and it is also around this age that babies begin to smile purposefully and even laugh out loud. This means that they are starting to interact more and are even starting to initiate interactions with adults. This is really quite amazing to most parents . . . a beautiful development to see. . . . Infants become more and more **sociable**. They will now smile at you when you smile at them, and it is very clear that many infants will **initiate** the smiling when someone comes up to them . . . in order to get that person to smile back at them . . . this means they are becoming very social, very interactive. . . . This is an important sign of development . . . one that encourages the adults around them to respond, giving babies even more reason to initiate, to interact!

OK, let's move on to four-month-old infants now. Infants around this age are starting to develop physically very quickly . . . some of them become very pudgy, almost fat around this age. What kinds of things is a four-month-old doing? Well, four-month-olds can usually roll over from their stomachs to their backs, and vice versa. This is great entertainment for them—they are finally getting mobile!

If you hold up four-month-old babies by their arms, you should notice that they are beginning to try to support themselves with their legs. Most babies at this age love to do this, to stand with support . . . this too gives them a great feeling of power . . . of control over their bodies. At this age babies also have very good neck and head control. And one other important thing—at four months, babies can now hold on to things that are put into their hands. As a matter of fact, four-month-old babies will often try to grab things lying within reach, anything within reach. Be careful! This includes your glasses, necklaces, and earrings!

And, as for their eyes, uh, at this point, they can follow faces and objects for a complete 180 degrees—that is, completely from far left to far right . . . 180 degrees. . . . Babies at this age will enjoy watching you as you move around the room, especially if you smile or wave at them.

What about language interaction? Wow! Their language has developed to a really delightful stage by this point. They laugh with delight quite often while playing—this is a true sign of interaction and social involvement. In fact, this is the age at which many adults make **silly sounds** and **make silly faces** at babies because they can get such a happy response. Four-month-olds also show excitement when they see their mothers or food by waving their arms and legs excitedly. This is clearly a wonderful time to visit a friend who has a baby because the baby is so much fun.

In terms of babies' **speech development**, those single-**syllable** vowel sounds that they made at two months have developed into combinations of two or more sounds like "eehooh" or "oohaah." This use of two or more syllables is a sign of language development . . . they are learning to control their speech more and are trying to **imitate** more and more.

Narrator: Stop the tape and answer the questions for Part 3. . . . Let's continue with the final section of the lecture. In this part, we will hear about the development of six-month-old infants.

PART 4

Well, this brings us to six months, which is as far as we'll go today. Motor skills, let's see . . . six-month-olds can generally sit up alone and, if you help pull them up and support them . . . or give them something to hang on to . . . they will be able to stand for a rather long time.

At this point, they support their weight with their legs. This is a major motor development. They are on their way to walking! They can roll around rather skillfully and some children may even be beginning to **crawl** a bit. What freedom for the baby . . . and what trouble for the parents!

Babies can, by this time, reach for and grasp an object that they want, and usually they want to grab whatever they see, not just toys! They can hold a toy in each hand now instead of having to drop one to hold the other as they have done in the past. This is another big development in motor control. In addition, they can move a toy from one hand to the other and, if you watch carefully, you'll probably find that they use both hands fairly equally. Hand preference doesn't show up until much later.

In terms of language and social development, a baby at this age will begin to respond by turning to look at you if you call his or her name. "Hi-la-ry"—the baby looks and smiles, and will often vocalize in return.

In terms of **productive** language ability, you'll notice that at six months babies begin to introduce a lot of **consonant sounds** into their vocabulary . . . like "ma" and "da." Before, you remember, they were using mostly vowel sounds—"ooh," "aah," and "eeh"—but now the consonant sounds are used regularly—"ma," "ba," "da," "ga," and so on. Most importantly . . . and take note of this, please . . . it is at this stage that babies begin to realize that saying certain sounds, like "ma," gets a predictable response from adults, particularly their mothers in this case. "She's saying mommy!!!" Talk about encouragement for the baby to continue developing language!

Significant social changes also start occurring in most six-month-olds. Babies begin to develop **preferences** . . . they like this toy more than that toy, they like this person but not that person, they want to be held by this person but not by that person, they want to eat this food but not that food . . . and so on. . . . For nearly everything, babies at this age seem to develop preferences . . . and when they don't get their preferences, what happens? You guessed it . . . **complaining** and **crying** and **fussing** . . . the babies' first fits.

Now, we have to remember that this is a very normal part of development. The baby has ways to show what he or she wants and likes . . . and so the mother and father should respond to this as a sign of development, not as a battle of wills. It's not really a challenge to the mother and father—just a healthy sign of development.

OK, well, we've gone to six months so I'll stop, but I hope this gives you some idea of the great beauty and excitement of this period of human development.

Narrator: Stop the tape and answer the questions for Part 4.

UNIT 11 The Disappearance of the Dinosaurs

Narrator: The lecture you are about to listen to concerns the dinosaurs and their sudden disappearance millions of years ago. In particular, it looks at a theory that attempts to explain this mystery, a theory that has been getting increasing support from the scientific community.

PART 1

OK everyone, I think most everyone has arrived, so let's begin. The subject of today's lecture is the dinosaurs, or more specifically, why the dinosaurs became **extinct**.

This is one of those topics that most people are usually pretty interested in: Why did the mighty dinosaurs disappear? I know that I've been interested in dinosaurs ever since I was five or six years old. I think that my interest as a child had to do with the fact that they were just awesome, enormous, and powerful creatures. They were the kind of thing you might find in a science fiction movie, but we know they actually existed here on Earth long before our time. . . . They not only existed, they were masters of the Earth until something—no one really can say for sure what—caused them to die out. And like I said, that's the subject of this lecture: What are the theories about their disappearance?

So, does anybody know when the dinosaurs died out to the nearest few million years or so, which is a rather short time in **paleontology**, after all? Well, it's generally thought to be about 65 million years ago. The dinosaurs, as a **species**, seem to have died out about 65 million years ago. This figure is the result of research by **geologists**, by **paleontologists**, and also by **archaeologists** who have found **fossils** and analyzed **rock formations** in different **strata**, different layers, of the **Earth's crust**.

Why the dinosaurs became extinct, why they died out, is a question that scientists have struggled with for years. At the present time, the most **widely held theory** suggests that **climatic changes**—changes in the climate of the Earth—caused the death of this giant species. These climatic changes were thought to have been caused by natural phenomena—some believe the most likely explanation is **volcanic activity** . . . volcanic eruptions around the Earth.

Many scientists, however, have felt that this solution is, well, inadequate to explain why dinosaurs all over the Earth became extinct at relatively the same time. They feel that the **Climatic Changes Theory** fails to account for the apparent speed with which the extinction took place. For millions of years the dinosaurs had existed and adapted to changing **environmental conditions**; indeed, the dinosaurs were surprisingly **adaptable** creatures. They had made changes before . . . relocating when a place became unfavorable. . . . So we must wonder: What event took place that was so **cataclysmic**, so catastrophic, that was so powerful, that it completely overwhelmed the entire species of dinosaurs? It's very hard to believe that volcanoes could have had this kind of immense power in more than just one region.

Narrator: Stop the tape and answer the questions for Part 1. . . . The lecturer now goes on to talk about a second theory that explains the disappearance of the dinosaurs.

PART 2

Well, there is another theory—let's call it the **Collision Theory**. It's an exciting theory that has recently been getting the respect and support of an increasing number of scientists, myself included. This theory claims that climatic changes were not directly responsible for the dinosaurs' extinction.

The new theory proposes instead that a **meteor**—perhaps 8 kilometers (about 5 miles) in diameter and traveling at 70 kilometers (about 44 miles) per second—**collided with** the Earth, hit the Earth with tremendous force and this disaster led to the end of the dinosaurs' reign over Earth.

Now, it's difficult for us to imagine the effects of such a collision, but scientists estimate that the meteor would have created a **crater** nearly 200 kilometers wide—that's about 130 miles wide. In addition, we can estimate that the impact would have forced about 1,700 cubic kilometers—or about 1,200 cubic miles—of **debris**, such as dust and dirt from the Earth, into the **atmosphere**. That's an awful lot of debris, and you might stop for a moment and consider just what effect all of that debris in the atmosphere might have had on life on Earth.

Of course, the large pieces would have quickly fallen back to Earth, but it's believed that the **finer particles** would have remained in the atmosphere and would have **blocked out sunlight** all over the world for months. These particles would then have fallen to Earth and formed a **layer of dust**. Because sunlight was blocked out for so long, the **Earth's temperature** would have dropped significantly, dropped by quite a lot, you see, and **photosynthesis**—the process whereby plants convert water and **carbon dioxide** into food and **oxygen** for life—photosynthesis would have at first slowed down and then eventually ceased or stopped altogether.

As you know, sunlight is essential to the process of photosynthesis, and photosynthesis is essential to the life of plants. Once photosynthesis stopped, many plants would have died and many of the creatures who depended on the plants for food, the dinosaurs among them, would also have perished. Plant-eating dinosaurs would not have survived. And here is the problem: The meat-eating dinosaurs generally fed on the plant-eating dinosaurs and, umm, they would . . . they would therefore simultaneously have lost their food source—the plant-eaters—and also have died out as a result. Obviously, the dinosaurs could never have survived this kind of disaster.

Narrator: Stop the tape and answer the questions for Part 2. . . . In the next section, some evidence or support for the theory is discussed.

PART 3

Now, if this picture is correct, an important question has to be answered: If a meteor did strike, then where is the **evidence**? How can we prove this actually happened? Where did the meteor strike? Well, after about a decade of searching, scientists think that this massive meteor may have struck on the northern tip of Mexico's **Yucatán Peninsula**. There, buried 1,100 meters (about 3,000 feet) below the ground, is a circular **basin** about 180 kilometers (about 113 miles) in diameter, about the size that I mentioned before. And the dating of nearby fossils has placed the crater's age . . . assuming it is a crater . . . to within 5 million years of the dinosaurs' extinction—very close in geological terms!

A couple more pieces of evidence that suggest a meteor may have been responsible must be mentioned. First of all, the **Cretaceous period** ended 65 million years ago. In the Cretaceous rock, there are fossils of dinosaurs and many other species. Above this Cretaceous rock is a thin layer of gray **clay** that has been found in sites all over the world. And above this is the rock of the **Tertiary period** in which—and this is important—there is no trace, I repeat, no trace, not one, of dinosaurs or any other Cretaceous species. As for the clay in between, it has been shown to contain a far higher content of the element **iridium** than is generally found in the Earth's crust. Why is this significant? Well, meteors have high iridium content. This suggests that the clay could have been formed by the worldwide **fallout** created by the collision of a meteor.

The second piece of evidence that supports the meteor theory is this: Samples taken from the basin—or crater, assuming a meteor hit—these **quartz crystal** samples taken from the crater have **striations** . . . uh, bands or **grooves**, that could only have been caused by powerful **shock waves** such as you might get from the great impact of a collision. These do not form from simple volcanic activity. This is the proof, if I may call it that, which is now available.

So, we have two pieces of hard evidence that support the meteor-collision theory. Interesting, isn't it? Well, there's some food for thought. I'm going to leave it there for today and say a bit more next class. Are there any questions about this right now?

Narrator: Stop the tape and answer the questions for Part 3.

UNIT 12 Fashion in the Twenty-first Century

Narrator: This is the kind of lecture you would hear in a fashion design course. This lecture concerns the types of fashions that may exist in the early twenty-first century.

PART 1

In today's lecture, I'm going to talk about fashions, and especially how fashions may change in the **clothing industry** over the next twenty years.

Clothing designers usually say that trying to predict fashion styles is like, well, like trying to predict how people will feel and think at a time in the **distant future**. In other words, it's almost impossible to do, although we can make some pretty good guesses, some educated guesses. So, I'm going to be guessing here with you today!

Our guesses are usually based on such things as, uh, the state of **technology** and **social trends**, as well as the fact that there tend to be certain **cycles** in fashion. As we all know, things periodically become **fashionable** only to later disappear again for a number of years. For instance, the width of men's ties seems to change at regular intervals, doesn't it? **Classical** styles, on the other hand, are influenced much less by the passage of time. They tend to remain well accepted for long periods of time, but even the classics may go by the wayside in the year 2000.

What I'd like to do, first of all, is tell you in general what **fashion designers** are predicting for the years 2000 and 2010 . . . in both **formal** and **informal** fashions. To finish with, I'll say a few words about changes in the **science** and technology of fashion that are likely to take place. And, as I think you'll see, technology will have a very **powerful influence** on fashions in the future, probably more powerful than in any time in the past.

Narrator: Stop the tape and answer the questions for Part 1. . . . Now let's continue with Part 2. In this section, we will hear about fashions for the years 2000 and 2010.

PART 2

So let's start with the year 2000. What kinds of clothes are setting the trend in the year 2000? Well, many designers say, and I agree with them, that clothing in the year

2000 is going to become more **functional** and high tech. For example, in order to help protect us against weather extremes, some fabrics will become **computerized**, or controlled by a tiny microprocessor, so that the wearer can adjust the temperature of the fabric to suit the weather conditions, perhaps with something like a **solar belt pack**. I suppose this idea is something like the electric blankets we have today—when it's cold you turn up the switch, when it's hot you turn down the switch. . . . In this type of clothing, the belt would have controls that would let the wearer adjust the amount of solar energy—energy from the sun—that would filter through the clothes. This would help control temperature. Finally, we may be seeing more **body paints**—a kind of underwear that we paint on ourselves to protect our bodies from the cold. These body paints will probably be available in different colors and textures, and people would wear them as a kind of **decoration**. Clearly, they would have both a **practical** use and be pretty at the same time.

As for the year 2010, many designers imagine that clothes will be designed to change color to suit the **surroundings** or **decor**—for example, they would turn white in sunlight, or turn blue in a blue room, or maybe they would change colors at the wearer's will. It may also be possible for clothes to change color according to the way a person feels. In other words, your shirt may turn red, for instance, if you feel angry, or your dress may turn yellow if you feel happy. Of course, the simplest way to do this is by making the clothing **sensitive** to **body temperature**. In any case, it's easy to imagine that some people might not like this kind of clothing—it would make it kind of hard to disguise your feelings! On second thought, this might not be such a good idea!

In a future that is more and more technologically **sophisticated**, our clothes may be one of the only means of **personal expression**. Big name designer lines may disappear and be replaced with clothes that are individually personalized before being manufactured.

Narrator: Stop the tape and answer the questions for Part 2. . . . Let's continue with Part 3. In this section, we will hear about styles for men and women.

PART 3

OK. Let's take a look for a moment at styles for men. I think we may see some big changes here. As far as styles for men are concerned, it seems that **traditional** clothing for men—the old pin-striped suits, button-down collars, and the traditional tie—will disappear altogether. Instead,

comfortable **sportswear** will be the **"in thing:"** Sportswear—more comfortable clothes—will become far more popular than it is even today. Light, **pastel-colored** clothes—light pinks and blues and yellows—which have been rather unpopular with men for centuries, will become more widely accepted. We can see that trend even now, especially among young men. In addition, men's clothes will probably become much looser than they are today . . . more closely resembling women's fashions. In fact, there will be a general tendency away from **sex specific** clothes, and so it is believed that men's clothes will be looser, showing more of the body. **Dress codes** will also largely disappear. In other words, uh, there may well be fewer **restrictions**, fewer limitations on what men can wear. What else? As part of this trend, skin creams, colognes, and other **cosmetics** for men will also grow in popularity. This is also in line with the notion that men's fashions will more closely resemble women's.

In the case of women, the biggest change in fashion will probably occur in business dress—as women assume more of a dominant position in the business world. In general, business wear for women will become more **conservative**. This tendency is therefore very different from what is expected of men's formal wear, almost the opposite of the trend in men's clothing. The change in women's clothing will actually be based largely on the growing power and influence of women in society.

Narrator: Stop the tape and answer the questions for Part 3. . . . Now, let's listen to Part 4 in which we will hear about the impact of science and technology on fashion.

PART 4

And finally, what is predicted for the roles of science and technology in fashion? How will science and technology influence fashion in the coming years? Well, it seems that advances in industrial technology will result in cheaper clothes, for one thing.

Clothing design will become computerized—**fabric selection**, length, size, color, and style will be **programmed** into a computer. Designers will then experiment with many alternatives before a final choice is manufactured. This will save a lot of time . . . you will be able to reject any design that you don't like before even one meter (about one yard) of cloth is used. Actually, this is already being done to some extent in Europe and other places . . . although it will no doubt become much more widespread in the near future.

Tailors and **seamstresses**, people who make clothes by measuring, cutting, and sewing fabrics, may lose their jobs as, instead of traditional tailoring and sewing, we begin to see **gluing** and **fusing**—that is, instead of thread, we will be using easier procedures to join pieces of cloth. Overall, these changes in the manufacturing process will be beneficial, I think. High quality and reasonable prices will make the whole fashion industry healthier.

Another area we should think about is **fabrics**, where we will be seeing less of **natural materials**—less cotton and wool, fewer furs . . . as these materials become less available and more protected. Instead, we are going to see **engineered fabrics**—more nylons and polyesters, and more **artificial** animal furs—all of different kinds, different colors, and different thicknesses. In addition, we are going to see much more in the way of paper clothes and other **"disposable"** clothes—you wear them and then throw them away. These might be especially useful for children. So, I think if you look at these ideas, you see a general movement toward practical, efficient clothing in the coming decades. Remember, though, this is all a guessing game. . . .

The real fashions of the coming years will probably incorporate some of these ideas, but I'm sure that there will be plenty of surprises!

All right, I'm going to leave it there. If anyone has any questions, I'll be happy to answer them now.

Narrator: Stop the tape and answer the questions for Part 4.